JOHANNES BOCKENHEIM

REGISTRUM COQUINE
A MEDIEVAL COOKBOOK

INTRODUCTION, TRANSLATION, AND GLOSSARY
BY MARCO GAVIO DE RUBEIS

First publication in 2021 by I Doni delle Muse

Copyright © 2021
by Historical Italian Cooking / I Doni delle Muse

Cover picture:
Miniature from "Le livre appellé Decameron" a Decameron translation by Laurent de Premierfait (15th century)

All rights reserved.
No part of this book may be reproduced, stored in a retrieval system, or transmitted, in any form or by any means, without the prior permission in writing of the publisher, nor be otherwise circulated in any form of binding or cover other than that in which it is published and without a similar condition including this condition being imposed on the subsequent purchaser.

INTRODUCTION

1. THE REGISTRUM COQUINE

The *Registrum Coquine* is a cookbook probably written in the first half of the 15th century (and surely, not before 1417) by a German cook and ecclesiastic, Johannes Bockenheim, who worked at the service of Pope Martin V according to the words of the author himself.

We know little about Bockenheim, except the few elements we mentioned, whereas we have more information about the pope he served, in his secular life named Oddone Colonna, though we ignore for how much time precisely. Even the period in which the two of them had met is unknown: we can guess that they knew each other around 1415, when the future pope was in Germany to participate in the Council of Constance.

It is possible that the *Registrum Coquine* was written after Martino's death in 1431, since the author states that he formerly worked as a cook under this pope, but we can not be sure about this, since Bockenheim could have left the pope's service when Martino was still alive.

Born around 1370, in the noble Colonna family, one of the most ancient and distinguished

Roman families, Oddone became pope with the name Martin V in a complicated and troubled period of the history of the church known as the Western Schism, lasted more than 40 years, to which he put an end. In this time, several popes and antipopes succeeded until his election in 1417; however, he could not come back to Rome before 1420 due to the complex political situation.

Martino V was intensely dedicated not only to the reconstruction of the church, but also to the arts and culture. Surely, his interest in cuisine, which is a fundamental cultural topic in the Middle Ages, reflects the personal attitudes of this great patron.

1.1 The manuscripts

Among the many medieval sources about cooking, the *Registrum Coquine* is quite peculiar for a series of elements that we will analyze. First of all, many recipes are simple and quick to prepare, differently from most that we read in other cookbooks written in the same period. Second, the author writes in Latin in a period in which the common tendency is to use vernacular languages, whereas Latin is more common in the older cookbooks.

Johannes von Bockenheim's Latin is poor, heavily influenced by Romance vernacular languages, possibly by Italian, and his directions are not always clear and easy to follow without the grammatical and logical analysis of the sentences, sometimes structured without consistency.

However, the use of few ingredients and the simplicity make this cookbook one of the easiest to study as a source for medieval cuisine and an excellent way to get started with a completely different way to experience food and cooking. A simplicity that does not bring to the sacrifice of the taste, since the recipes are excellent and delicious.

Another characteristic of this book is that all the recipes are suggested to specific social classes or nationalities. We can not know for sure how much Bockenheim's directions mirror reality at his time; anyway, this cookbook is a precious source of information about elements that would be, otherwise, lost and essential to anyone who want to know better the culinary culture in the Middle Ages.

Two manuscripts survived of the *Registrum Coquine*, each one with specific characteristics and clearly written by different persons: not only there are a few recipes that do not appear in both the books, but the lexicon shows some variations (for example, to mean saffron, one always uses the term *crocus*; the other *zapharano,* with a few spelling variants).

To simplify our work, we will call them manuscripts A and B. Manuscript A is collected in the Bibliothèque Nationale de France (Ms Latin 7054); manuscript B is part of the Segal collection and we find it in the Bibliothèque Internationale de Gastronomie at Lugano.

To write this book, we mainly used manuscript B, more interesting for the variety of social classes represented, and amended the evident mistakes using the other manuscript when it was needed. Most recipes are the same, but some appear just in one of them. We divided our translation into two parts: the first includes the recipes from manuscript B, with the most significant variants from the other manuscript; in the second part you will find the recipes present just in manuscript A.

There are a few differences in the language used in the two manuscripts. In the glossary at the end of this book, you will find the lexicon of manuscript B, with the addition of some of the words present in the other edition.

1.2 Recipes and social classes

As mentioned before, one of the most fascinating features of this cookbook is that the author recommends the various recipes to specific social groups or nationalities. Actually, there is nothing new in this, since medieval authors have always the tendency to attribute the various foods to different groups of people. We find similar suggestions in a few books, including *Anonimo Toscano*, the *Tractatus de Modo Condiendi et Preparandi Omnia Cibaria*, and the *Liber de Coquina*, as well as in several medical treatises.

The idea that a specific time of the year and region of the world require a peculiar diet, as well as the complexion, the job, or the physical activity, has a long tradition. We find this concept in older medical sources, in particular the *Corpus Hippocraticum* and Galen's dietetic works, as well as in the medieval books. People who make great physical efforts need a diet completely different from, for example, a scholar or a noble. The daily activity, as well as the exercise, partially modifies the complexion that, according to the humoral medicine, belongs to each individual, but it is fundamental to remember that season, age, place, and even time of the day tend to change the specific needs.

According to ancient and medieval medicine, the diet must be diversified considering all the variables, and the physician has the important task to evaluate the physical condition and reckon which foods and beverages are more suitable for a specific person.

Bockenheim does not consider the medical aspects, just the gastronomic ones, but it is important to know the cultural foundations from which this book originates. In the *Registrum Coquine*, we read that cow meat is good for peasants, but it is nothing new: many centuries before, Galen wrote that this kind of meat is suitable for the ones who make great physical efforts, as the athletes (*De Facultatibus Alimentorum*, 1.1).

In *Anonimo Toscano*'s manuscript, we find a recipe with turnips, saffron, and beef intended for the *comune famiglia*, a term that, as well as ancient Roman *familia*, includes the servants. To understand how the food was perceived in the Middle Ages, this fact is essential: it means that an Italian professional cook lived in the 14th century, such as this anonymous author, considered a dish prepared with these ingredients nothing special, but on the contrary, an everyday meal for common people. We will find many other similar examples in Bockenheim's work.

The most significant difference between the two manuscripts of the *Registrum Coquine* is for which social groups the recipes are meant, more diverse in the one we chose for this book, whereas manuscript A focuses more on the populations and less on the social classes.

Clearly, we do not know with certainty whether Bockenheim's directions corresponded to reality and, for example, peasants and farmers actually ate the foods he describes, but we must always remember that we are reading a source written by a professional cook, who surely knew his social context and the world of his time, at least for what concerns the alimentary habits.

Moreover, confronting the information that we find in this and other cookbooks with the medical sources, we find similar suggestions, as we will analyze below in our book. As a consequence, we should read the *Registrum Coquine* with attention, as a testimony of a Middle Age quite different from the common biased view.

In manuscript B, we find 13 recipes for the rich, nobles, princes (*magnates*, *principi*, *divites*, *nobili*); 7 recipes for people who live in the countryside and peasants (*rustici* and *villani*), very simple and with a scarce use of spices; a couple of recipes for pimps (*lenoni*) and prostitutes (*meretrices* and *mulieres eorum*, referring to *lenoni*); two for monks and religious (*moniales*, *monachi*, *religiosi*); one for actors (*hystriones*); one for women (*mulieres*); one for notaries and copyists (*notarii* and *copisti*); one for soldiers or mercenaries (*stipendiarii*); one each for laics and priests (*laici* and *famuli*). In addition, as common in the medieval cookbooks, there are two recipes for the sick in the section dedicated to the lean recipes for Lent.

Among the nationalities to which the various recipes are suggested, we find Alemanni, Marcomanni, Bohemians, Suevians, Saxons, Hungarians, Gauls, Angles, but also Italics (sometimes, specifically Romans), and several others.

It is interesting to notice that what distinguishes the recipes for the nobles and the ones for the plebeians is, first of all, the different complexity and, frequently, just the kind of meat (for example, pheasants and capons are consumed by the higher classes).

About the spices, we will analyze more their use according to the various authors in a paragraph below. The diffusion of spices across the different social classes is confirmed by many sources, providing in this way a fascinating and complex vision of how people ate in the Middle Ages. Spices appear in the recipes for both the lower and higher classes, with a couple of important differences: the quantity and the quality, two factors that have a great influence on the final cost of the dishes.

1.3 Lean days and fat days

This cookbook is divided into three parts, titled *Registrum Coquine*, *Registrum Coquine in Quadragesima*, and *Registrum de Piscibus*. These, roughly, correspond to the sections dedicated to the lean days and fat days. The clear division between the fat days and lean days is essential in medieval culture, and its importance, partially, will continue in the following centuries.

In the Middle Ages, several days of the year belonged to the so-called lean days, which were days of penitence and fast. Johannes Bockenheim, as a clergy man and cook, had to consider them to arrange banquets fit for the specific time of the year. The lean periods par excellence were Lent and all the Fridays, with the addition of other days during the year. In the recipes for the lean days, not only meat is absent, but also butter, cheese, milk, and eggs, substituted with almond milk and butter, olive oil, and fish.

Fish is the specific food for Lent and the lean days, in addition to various vegetables and legumes, considered suitable for penitence and maceration. In the monastic rules, we find more or less lean days, depending on the order, and in a few cases, for example the Benedictine rule, we read that meat is usually forbidden, save in case of sickness or elder age and with the exception of a few festivities. This is due to the fact that the life of a monk must be a life of penance, and the abstinence from meat is considered a harsh form of atonement in the medieval culture, a fact that hints at the common use of meat in that period.

In the lists of the plates in the Renaissance sources, we find more and more dairy products served during the lean days, with the common exception of Lent, with a gradual decrease of the limitations in the choice of foods throughout the centuries, a sign of a more limited influence of the religion upon the daily life and therefore, the diet.

In any case, it is clear that fish, habitually, was

not appreciated in the Middle Ages as it was in ancient times, in which saltwater fish was very costly and prized. The medieval cookbooks mainly present recipes with freshwater fish, and the *Registrum Coquine* is not an exception.

In this book, there are more recipes for the fat days than for the lean days, as common in the medieval sources, and frequently, the lean recipes offer a fat version. A few fat recipes can easily turn into lean ones just by substituting the animal fats with olive oil. In manuscript B, there are 52 fat recipes (among which 13 without meat, except for broth or lard which may be substituted); 10 recipes for vegetables, fruit, and legumes; 8 recipes for fish; and 4 recipes for sauces (with just one in which the author uses offal and meat). To these ones, we must add 5 fat recipes, 2 lean recipes, and just one fish recipe from manuscript A.

Among the lean and meatless recipes, we listed a few with meat broth, that can be easily substituted with almond milk, a very common ingredient in this cookbook.

2. THE OTHER SOURCES FOR THIS BOOK

We wrote this book for all enthusiasts and curious interested in the history of gastronomy, who want to read an original source directly without having to struggle against great difficulties in the interpretation. We did not intend this book for scholars and specialists, but for everyone who desires to approach historical food in both theoretical and practical ways, the reason why we added suggestions about how to prepare the recipes described here. We believe that the best way to know the history of food is by trying it, following our taste and inspiration, to bring the past back to life through the direct experience.

In addition to the translation of the recipes, we wrote a short comment to help to understand the passages that seem more difficult to interpret and the various steps of the recipes, not always clear, sometimes using other sources to better clear up the text. Medieval cuisine must ever be put in context, and it is necessary to broaden our knowledge through the reading of the other sources.

As for our other books, we chose to rely on primary sources exclusively, using our own translations, a method that we consider the only one suitable to discover the historical truth and reduce the inevitable mistakes and interpretative misunderstandings. Frequently, the approach toward history, in particular medieval history, is clouded by biases and preconceptions that must be, as much as possible, put aside when we read the original texts.

We consider it the best way to discover the authentic reality beyond the veil of the past. Clearly, this method does not eliminate possible misreadings, but the reflection about the text, the analysis of the lexicon, the comparison with other sources are the best ways to limit them, at least partially.

For this book, we focused on Italian sources. Despite being Bockenheim a German cook, indeed, we know that he worked in Italy, possibly in Rome, and he surely knew most of the cookbooks available at his time.

There are a few fundamental sources to better understand medieval cooking and, more specifically, the *Registrum Coquine*. We will now briefly describe the most important that we used among the cooking and dietetic books.

2.1 Ancient sources

Despite many ancient sources have been forgotten during the Middle Ages, ancient Roman texts are still fundamental for medieval culinary culture, especially the books of agriculture and Pliny's *Naturalis Historia*: Cato's *De Agri Cultura*, Columella's *De Re Rustica*, and Palladius' *Opus Agriculturae*.

To the same tradition are connected two relevant sources written in a later period: a 10th-century Byzantine collection, titled *Geoponics*, in which are present texts written by various authors, and *Ruralia Commoda* by Pietro de' Crescenzi, dating back to the 13th or 14th century, which will follow the model of the ancient agricultural authors, in particular Palladius and Columella. There had been several editions and reprints of this book throughout the centuries, both in Latin and vernacular.

Other essential texts are the cookbook conventionally attributed to Marcus Gavius Apicius, *De Re Coquinaria*, and Athenaeus' *Deipnosophists*, a book that collects several quotes and recipes mainly written by Greek cooks.

2.2 Cookbooks

There are plenty of cookbooks written in the Middle Ages, in particular starting from the 14th century.

The most important books are two, both written in Latin around the end of the 13th century or the beginning of the 14th: the *Tractatus de Modo Preparandi et Condiendi Omnia Cibaria*, a complete treatise about medieval food from which the later sources will take inspiration, and the *Liber de Coquina*. These two books are complementary and essential to understand the basics of medieval cuisine, especially in Italy.

In addition, we used the two books conventionally called *Anonimo Toscano*, which are mainly translations into Tuscan vernacular of the *Liber de Coquina*, with interesting changes and additions, dating back to the 14th century. Belonging to the same period is another fascinating source, called *Anonimo Fiorentino*. Other important books are *Anonimo Meridionale* and *Anonimo Veneziano*, written around the end of the 14th century. All these cookbooks are written in vernacular.

Two cookbooks more are worth to be mentioned. The first is the work by Maestro

Martino in the second part of the 15th century (later than the *Registrum Coquine*), titled *Libro de Arte Coquinaria*, which has a couple of recipes in common with Bockenheim's book. The second was written by the most famous 16th-century Italian cook, Bartolomeo Scappi, which helps to shed light on basic preparations whose recipes were clearly given for granted by the medieval authors, for example how to make the crusts for the pies or how to prepare various kinds of pasta.

2.3 Dietetic books and other sources

The medical sources are fundamental to understand the principles at the basis of medieval dietetics, built upon older traditions, in particular the works by Hippocrates, Galen (mainly *De Facultatibus Alimentorum*), and Dioscorides (*Materia Medica*).

One of the oldest medieval books is *De Observatione Ciborum*, which dates back to the 6th century, written by the Byzantine physician Anthimus. The book, written in Latin, is addressed to the king of the Franks and contains not only dietetic suggestions but also recipes. The text collects important information about the diet of the Franks, among whom the author worked during a period of his life.

Then, there is *De Flore Dietarum*, an 11th-century booklet that belongs to the tradition of the Salernitan Medical School, which on its turn synthesizes and collects medical traditions coming from Arabic and Greek authors. In this book, we find detailed information about the aliments and some recipes, in addition to suggestions about how to cook foods in order to make them healthier. To the same tradition belongs the medical work by Arnaldo de Villa Nova (13th or 14th century) and the *Regimen Sanitatis Salernitanum* (11th century), to which Arnaldo dedicates an important commentary.

A text we used for this book is halfway between a dietetic treatise and a cookbook (a very short one): Mainus de Maineris' *Opusculum de Saporibus*, which explains how to prepare healthy sauces, providing the theoretical basis for the cooks and physicians.

It is essential, then, Michele Savonarola's book, titled *Trattato Utilissimo di Molte Regole per conservare la Sanità, dichiarando qual cose siano utili da mangiare et quali triste: et medesimamente di quelle che si bevono per Italia* ("very useful treatise about the many rules to keep good health, stating which things are useful to eat and which harmful, and at the same time, which things are drunk in Italy"). This book was reprinted several times. We are using here the edition issued in Venice in 1590, to testimony the long fortune of this 15th-century treatise even after the end of the Renaissance.

The peculiarity of this book is that the author not only writes about several kinds of foods and beverages (among which cereals, bread, legumes, fruit, meat, fish, eggs, dairy products, wine), but also helps us to contextualize their use according to the social classes and, clearly, provides information about the healthier ways to cook them (sometimes in contrast with unhealthy habits that Savonarola describes in detail, showing how the foods were commonly prepared at his time).

This text is dedicated to Savonarola's liege, Niccolò d'Este, Marquis of Ferrara, to whom the author frequently refers directly, and is essential to learn the ways a medieval physician looked upon the foods and alimentary uses of his contemporary age.

De Honesta Voluptate et Valetudine by Bartolomeo Sacchi, called Platina, is half-way between a cookbook and a dietetic treatise, with a large part dedicated to translations into Latin of Maestro Martino's cookbook, written instead in vernacular. The text dates back to the 15th century. We used the edition printed in 1538.

Another source we used is the commentary to Dioscorides' *Materia Medica* written by the 16th-century physician Pietro Andrea Mattioli, in which there are information that complete and explain passages from other medical texts. Despite being written later, this book is essential to understand the continuity of ancient medicine throughout the centuries.

Following the index of the medical work by Dioscorides, Mattioli's commentary explains the various entries adding information about the usage of the ingredients at his times or in ancient and medieval periods, adding observations that compare the opinions of other physicians. This book too was reprinted several times.

The last source we mention is not really a dietetic book, but the work of a 16th-century naturalist, Costanzo Felici, in which the author writes about vegetables, fruit, spices, and cereals, with useful information about how vegetables were used and by which social classes. This short book is titled *Dell'Insalata e Piante che in Qualunque Modo Vengono per Cibo dell'Homo* ("about the salads and all plants that in any way are used as foods by people").

3. INGREDIENTS AND BASIC METHODS

As we mentioned above, the *Registrum Coquine* is different from the cookbooks of the same period, and one of its characteristics is the use of fewer ingredients for the recipes, frequently simpler than the ones written by other authors.

In this chapter, we will write about the ingredients, analyzing them with the help of texts written by cooks and physicians, to put them into context. We will also explain the basic preparations that the author gave for granted, but are essential to recreate the recipes as he intended them, using passages selected from the sources mentioned in the latter chapter.

3.1 Cereals and seeds

Cereals are quite rare in this cookbook, in which we mainly find recipes for meat and cheese, with a few methods for fish, eggs, and vegetables. There is just one recipe for spelt in both the manuscript and one for rice in manuscript A, substituted in the other edition with a recipe for nigella seeds. Moreover, there is a further recipe with hemp seeds.

In the *Registrum Coquine* there are no pasta recipes, just methods for two different kinds of pies, called *torta* and *pastillum, basteda* in manuscript A. Below, we will explain how to prepare them.

Despite their scarce presence in this cookbook, cereals are worth to be examined, as well as the basic methods to use them, in particular to make bread, a staple ingredient in the Middle Ages which was prepared in various ways.

Bread. Starting from ancient Greece, the kind of bread, considered the best and most nutritious has always been white wheat bread, salted and well leavened, as we read in several sources, for example the *Regimen Sanitatis Salernitanum* and *De Flore Dietarum*. However, there were many kinds of bread in the Antiquity and Middle Ages. Michele Savonarola writes about this topic extensively (5r).

"About wheat bread. There are three kinds of wheat bread; first, the one made with superfine wheat flour [*fiore de formento*], then a half-way kind made with a lot of bran [*del mezan cioe con molta remola*], then a third made with scarce bran [*il terzo cioe con poca remola*]. The first is good, temperate, and excellent. It is a bread suitable for princes and great masters [*pan da principi e da gran maestri*]: when it is made with good wheat, well cooked, well leavened [*ben cotto, ben levato*], with all its harmful humors removed, it nourishes well and is digested easily. As Avicenna says, it helps to gain weight soon, in particular if freshly prepared. The bread made with oil allows to put on a lot of weight. Your grace may use this one."

It is important to avoid eating bread still hot, since it causes damage to the teeth and gums, the author continues. In addition, bread must be not too hard nor unleavened. To remove its potential harm, Savonarola suggests adding salt and fennel seeds. Salt, indeed, consumes the humidity and makes the bread lighter and easier to digest, as well as tastier.

The second kind of bread (5v) contains a lot of bran and it is called *pan da cane* (bread for dogs). From Savonarola's words, it is evident that this is not a kind of bread commonly eaten. "The second bread with a lot of bran is hard to digest and is a good bread for a strong, hot stomach [*pan bon per i stomachi caldi e forti*], especially if it is eaten a huge quantity. But a small quantity at the beginning of the meal, just two or three morsels, in particular to the one who has a humid stomach, does not cause harm."

The third kind is made with less bran and is easier to digest than the second. It is bread for common people [*da comuna zente*] and is hard to digest but less than the one mentioned above. Like the first one, it must be well cooked and well leavened not to cause harm [*e quando non e ben cotto e ben levato (...) fa i nocumenti sopraditti*].

Wheat is not the only cereal used for bread. According to Savonarola (6r), spelt is another good cereal to make bread, being its characteristics similar to wheat. The author lists then breads made with barley, common millet, foxtail millet, sorghum, rye, fava beans, and even chestnuts, but these are not for courtiers. This information is important to us, since we can use these kinds of flour when we prepare recipes not meant for the rich or in which Bockenheim does not specify that the bread must be white, which always means made with white wheat flour.

As we read before, the best bread is well leavened; as a consequence, yeast is a fundamental ingredient. In the medieval sources, the methods to prepare it are given for granted. In any case, we know that back then there were at disposal manuscripts of the works of Pliny (18.26) and Palladius (11.21), who refer the ancient methods to make yeast by kneading millet flour or bran with grape must fermented for three days and shaping small cakes (called *mustei*) dried and meant to be preserved for the whole year.

Another method was to keep aside a piece of unsalted dough or a piece of the dough of the previous day, according to Pliny, who also describes two kinds of sourdough in the same chapter. Sourdough is mentioned by medieval authors, for example the Arabic physician Mesue and the Byzantine Aetius of Amida, whereas the use of *mustei* or even fresh must directly, a technique described by both Pliny (18.27) and Cato (121), is reported in the *Geoponics* (2.33).

Torta and pastillum. In the manuscripts, including the *Registrum Coquine*, there are plenty of recipes for *torte* and *pastelli*, two different kinds of pies, but with scarce information about how to make the crusts, given for granted by the authors. To know something more, we need to read other late-medieval and Renaissance sources.

There is just a direct reference to the crusts for a *pastillum* in the *Registrum Coquine*, and we find it in manuscript A, in which the author suggests using bread dough. In manuscript B, instead, there are no specific directions about this (32). In any case, from this passage, we know that it is correct to use bread dough when we make a Bockenheim's *pastillum*, as well as regular kinds of crusts.

Reading the other sources, however, we find further information. The basic recipe for the crust of the two pies is the same: knead flour and water until you obtain a smooth consistency, then roll the crusts; thick for the *pastillum*, thin for the *torta*. The crust for the *torta* must be similar to lasagna, a plate very popular in the Middle Ages, though it does not appear in this cookbook.

However, sometimes the recipes are more complex. To the crust for the *pastillum*, indeed, there are plenty of other ingredients to add: fats (butter, lard, or for the lean days, almond butter and olive oil), eggs, spices (in particular saffron to give a yellow color to the crust), rose water, and others. It is important to notice that, frequently, *pastillum* is made with a hole on top to pour liquids during the cooking, a technique not used for the *torta*.

To make the *torta*, the ingredients are similar, usually without fats. In *Anonimo Veneziano*'s manuscript, we find the suggestion to use saffron and spices to make the crusts, as well as herb juice.

About the crust for the *pastillum*, there are a few recipes for *pasticcio* in the book of Bartolomeo Scappi, written in the 16th century. Scappi describes a very simple crust with just flour and water (5.1), then writes about other kinds of crusts (5.10).

"Have prepared a crust made with flour, egg yolks, a bit of lard, and salt, and in this crust place the filling in such a way it takes the shape of a pyramid to keep the lid lifted [*si metti la compositione ricolta, di modo che venga sù dritta a foggia d'una piramide, questo si fa acciocche tenga sollevato il coperchio*]. Cover the *pasticcio* and cook it in the oven. When it will be almost cooked through, pour in the hole on top beaten egg yolks, clear verjuice, and a bit of broth. This *pasticcio* needs to be cooked at low heat. If it takes too much color, cover it with a double layer of paper [*se pigliasse troppo colore di sopra, cuoprirsi con un foglio di carta straccia doppio*]. And make this with the other *pasticci* if they take too much color."

Below in the text (5.47), then, Scappi describes another recipe and suggests mixing "flour, egg yolks, rose water, salt, and warm water. For each pound of dough, take eight ounces of butter and add it a little at a time to the dough, kneading all the time until the butter is finished [*mescolando del continuo sino a tanto che sia finito il butiro*]."

Butter is not very common in the oldest medieval high-end cooking recipes, but becomes frequent in the Renaissance and is used by Bockenheim, as we will see in the paragraph dedicated to the cooking fats.

Spelt. In the Italian medieval sources, spelt seems mainly used to make soups and pies, but we know from Savonarola's book that spelt bread was quite common.

In the *Registrum Coquine*, it is used for two recipes: in one, it is an ingredient to make meatballs (54); in the other, to make a soup for the sick (61). Among the ancient Roman recipes, we find a few methods similar to the one of recipe 54: for example, Cato's *globi* (79) and Apicius' *farcimina* (2.5). The first are fritters made with spelt and cheese; the latter, sausages filled with several ingredients, among which spelt.

The use of spelt for the sick is, instead, typically medieval. We find it, for example, in *Anonimo Toscano*'s manuscript (in which it is cooked with almond milk, egg yolks, saffron, sugar, and salt) as well as in the dietetic book by Savonarola (6r), who states that sugar removes its viscosity and is a good food for the sick [*et e cibo bono per gli infermi*]. The physician, as well as the ancient authors, distinguishes between *farro* and *spelta*, writing that the latter must be eaten adding not only sugar, but also ground anise seeds (6v).

Rice. Rice appears in one recipe reported in manuscript A. It is quite common in the medieval cookbooks, both the grains and flour, to prepare soups and other dishes. The best way to prepare rice, according to many authors, is by cooking it twice, first in water and then in almond milk, at low heat, with sugar. This method is reported by both *Anonimo Veneziano* and *Anonimo Fiorentino*, but it is the same technique described by Anthimus who, however, suggests overcooking the rice until it dissolves. Sugar is absent in Anthimus' recipe (7C).

Savonarola (10r) recommends adding almond milk or fat meat, but considers it harmful to use sheep milk as, instead, suggested in the *Registrum Coquine*.

Nigella and hemp seeds. In this cookbook, there are two recipes with seeds. The ingredients are worth to be examined. Nigella and hemp are used here to make soups, though both of them are scarcely present in the medieval cookbooks. The very limited use of hemp is confirmed by Pietro Andrea Mattioli (3.159-160), who writes that the seeds are roasted and pounded, then used at the end of the meal to drink more [*sono alcuni, che l'usano abbrustolato, e pesto nella fine della mensa, per poter meglio bevere*].

Hemp appears in two recipes for the lean days written by Maestro Martino, around the end of the 15th century, both very simple.

To make the first, the author recommends soaking the seeds in water for one day and one night, removing the ones floating on top. Then, this is the preparation: "take well-peeled almonds and pound them with the seeds mentioned above. Once they are well ground, dilute with fresh water and good pea broth, adding fine sugar and a bit of rose water. Then, cook all these ingredients for 1/8 of an hour, more or less, stirring all the time with the spoon."

The other recipe, instead, is a typical soup, with layers of liquids alternated with layers of toasted bread: "simmer for a short time the seeds, until they start breaking, then pound them in the mortar with peeled almonds, diluting with fresh water and sifting the milk obtained in this way. Then, boil the milk with a bit of salt and enough sugar, adding pepper if you like it [*un poco di pepe si al gusto ti piace*], boiling then again for the time needed for a *Miserere* [*un'altra volta lo lassarai bollire per spatio quanto diresti un miserere*]. Then, cut a loaf of bread into slices and roast them for a while, arranging them on a plate. Pour over the hemp milk and pay attention that the bread does not break [*vota fora tutto il ditto lacte regendo il pane che non si sconci*]. Pour again the milk two or three times, then serve the soup dusted with sweet spices."

Nigella is quite rare as a cooking ingredient: the *Registrum Coquine* is one of the few medieval sources that mention it. According to Pietro Andrea Mattioli (3.87), it was widely used in Germany [*frequentissimo si ritrova in Alemagna*], and this is maybe one of the reasons why Bockenheim includes a nigella recipe in his cookbook. In manuscript A, this recipe is substituted with another with rice, very similar.

3.2 *Vegetables, legumes, and fruit*

There are few vegetables in the *Registrum Coquine*, just garlic, onions, leeks, turnips, and spinach.

Garlic. We find garlic in two recipes of the *Registrum Coquine*. According to *De Flore Dietarum*, leeks, garlic, and onions cause headaches. Since the Antiquity, it was considered a plebeian food. It is mentioned, for example, in the pseudo-Vergilian *Moretum*, written around the 1st century, in which the main character, a farmer, eats a mixture of cheese, garlic, and aromatic herbs with wheat flatbread. In *De Re Coquinaria*, instead, garlic appears just in one recipe for cumin sauce, meant to help digestion (9.13). Its use to comfort the stomach is confirmed also by Anthimus, a few centuries later (62).

The poor reputation of garlic is given by its strong flavor, cursed by the farmer of the *Moretum*; however, in the medieval sources, it is used by both nobles and common people, though Michele Savonarola (15v) writes that it is the ginger of the peasant [*e zenzeuro da vilano*].

In the 11th tale by Giovanni Sercambi, collected in the *Novelliere* (beginning of the 15th century), a peasant is given to eat millet bread, cold fava beans, two heads of garlic, and leeks (and he is so famished that these poor foods seem as good as a ham to him), accompanied with wine, instead of the better foods his host has prepared and hidden before: capon, chicken *pastello* [*grosta di pollastro*], and focaccia with cheese [*fogaccia incaciata*].

In the *Registrum Coquine*, it appears in a recipe for a garlic-based soup (70), unsurprisingly meant for peasants, and in another for a stuffed goose (44), a dish that we find eaten by common people, for example in the *Trecentonovelle* by Franco Sacchetti (186), in which the goose is meant to be filled with either quinces or garlic.

Onion. Onions are quite common in the medieval cookbooks, used as a condiment but also to make soups and pies. According to Michele Savonarola (15r-15v), there are several kinds of onions, red and white, round and elongated. The author provides interesting information about which social classes should use them; however, considered the huge presence of onions in the high-end medieval cuisine, it is clear that this kind of advice was generally ignored.

They are unsuitable for scholars and doctors [*non è pasto da doctori né da quelli che hano adoperare molto qualsiasi studio*], writes Savonarola, because they cloud the intellect [*offusca lo intelletto*], and they must be forbidden to falconers [*comanda a tuoi falconieri non usino la cipolla*], because they dim the sight [*scurisse il vedere*], but on the contrary, they must be given to strong people.

Pietro Andrea Mattioli lists the many varieties of onions (2.150): big, small, elongated, round, flat, red, green, the same color as the skin, white, sweet, half-way between sweet and pungent, pungent [*di grosse, e di picciole, di lunghe, di tonde, e di schiacciate, di rosse, di verdi, e d'incarnate, e di bianche, di dolci, di mediocri e d'acute se ne trovano*]. Among the onions there are also shallots, cultivated since ancient Rome.

Leek. The leeks, according to Savonarola (16r), are as harmful to the intellect as the onions; however, one can remove the potential damage dressing them with oil, vinegar, and salt, or simmering them with fat meat and fennel or root parsley. Leeks are, besides, good for singers since they make the voice clearer, as we find recommended in the *Naturalis Historia* by Pliny as the favorite remedy used by Emperor Nero (19.33).

In the *Registrum Coquine*, leeks are used to make a soup for Lent (53), with a variant for the fat days with meat broth. The use of leeks with fat broth or meat, fresh or salted, or with almond milk like in the *Registrum Coquine*, is rather common in the medieval recipes, and this dish, similar to the one described by Savonarola, is called *porrata*.

Turnip. Since the Antiquity, turnips have been considered a food for farmers (and the turnip recipe in manuscript A is, indeed, a soup for peasants) but we find them in high-cooking recipes, starting from *De Re Coquinaria*. In the medieval cookbooks, there are both the roots and tops of the turnips, frequently to make soups and preserves, according to the ancient tradition.

Costanzo Felici describes several kinds of turnips: white, round, but also flattened; small and big and half-way; with an elongated [*longhe*] or an oval [*ovate*] form. The big and flattened are more appreciated for their tender pulp. They are used both raw and cooked to prepare salads, soups, and other plates, but also alone, very common in particular in the countryside [*si magna cotta e cruda in insalata, in minestra, in altre vivande e per se stessa et è cibo molto frequente e principalmente nella villa*]. The leaves and tender tops are eaten in soups. Turnip salads are dressed with concentrated grape juice [*sapa*], vinegar, and pepper.

The proper way to cook turnips and make them well nourishing, we read in *De Flore Dietarum* and again in Michele Savonarola's book (28v), consists in simmering them two times, discarding the water of the first cooking and boiling them again with fat meat [*si coquantur in aqua illaque proiecta, in alia recoquantur cum pingui carne, bene nutriunt*], a method quite common in medieval cuisine, but not followed by Bockenheim. Other ways to prepare turnips, Savonarola adds, are to roast or preserve them with vinegar, honey, fennel, and cumin to remove the potential harm.

Spinach. The spinach appear in two recipes of the *Registrum Coquine* (54 and 66). Michele Savonarola (11r-11v) describes a method very similar to recipe 54: spinach are good against red choler and must be cooked in water, then discarded. After that, they are fried in a pan with almond oil, adding then cinnamon. The recipe is recommended for the ones who have hot chest and lungs. Savonarola uses good and fresh almond oil, whereas Johannes Bockenheim almond milk, but the principles are the same.

The other recipe for spinach in the *Registrum Coquine* is even simpler than that, with spinach stir-fried with oil and dressed with vinegar, salt, and spices.

Writes Costanzo Felici that the tender leaves are used raw in salads, but it is more common to cook them in soups, pies, and other foods for the days before the holidays [*alle volte vole intrare in queste insalate con le sue foglie tenere, ma è più in uso al tempo della vigilia cotta in minestra et in torte magre et altri cibi*].

Peas. Among the recipes for the lean days, we find one recipe for fava beans and one for peas, both dry. There are many recipes for legumes in the medieval cookbooks, for the lean and the fat days, as well as in the ancient sources.

We find scarce information about peas in the medieval books. Pietro de Crescenzi (3.20) writes in his *Ruralia Commoda* that there are two kinds of pea, also called *roviglia* in the sources (spelled in several ways), one black and the other white. The author considers them better than fava beans, since they do not bloat and produce good humors, recommending them in particular in summer and in the hot regions.

Savonarola (8v) recalls that in his city, Ferrara, peas are called *bisi*, a name still used in some Italian regions. He considers that the best are the big and fresh peas; however, they are hard to digest.

Fava beans. The anonymous author of *De Flore Dietarum* distinguishes between two kinds of fava beans [*faba*], one of them big and white [*faba magna et alba*], considering the latter healthier than the first, in particular if husked, cooked two times in water, and seasoned with pepper, cumin, and lard. Michele Savonarola agrees with the opinion that the big and white fava beans are better; however, he considers any kind of *fava* a food for peasants [*pasto da vilano*, 6r-v].

Fava beans, the physician adds, must be prepared as for *De Flore Dietarum*, then mashed and seasoned with salt, pepper, sage, and oil. In this way, they give good nourishment. Lately in Ferrara, people use to eat a lot of fresh *fava*, and worse, with salted cheese, a deplorable habit [*ma ultimamente qui recordaro la destestanda consuetudine di Ferara, che tanta fava frescha manzano, e pezo con il formaio salato*] which causes illness and even death. Possibly, the author adds, this is the reason why there are so many sick in the city.

In the medieval sources, there are several recipes for this legume, both fresh and dried, to make pies and soups, and many dishes are prepared with methods similar to the ones described above by the physicians, not too different from how they were cooked in the Antiquity (for example, *De Re Coquinaria*, 5.4).

Fruit. In the medieval cookbooks, recipes based on fresh fruit are quite rare, except for some fritters, pies, preserves, and candies. Dry fruit and nuts, instead, are frequent, in particular almonds and raisins.

Apples. Apples are among the most used kinds of fruit. Costanzo Felici describes several varieties, both sweet and sour. "Apples [*mele*], also called *pomum* (in Latin, though the correct plural form would be *poma*), are a very common food, available almost all the year [*cibo molto frequente alla gente et quasi d'ogne stagione*], both ripe and unripe. People eat them raw and cooked on the fire or oven, and use them to make plates like soups, pies, roasts, and sauces [*vivande como minestre et torte e in arrosti e guazzetti*]. In the countries in which the grapes are scarce, people use apples to prepare wine in the same way as they do with pears. There are so many varieties that I can not list even half of them.

The cultivated kinds are several. Their shapes are elongated, round, or flat [*longhe o tonde o piatte*]; their colors, intense red, clear red, green-red, green, yellow, white, rust, and others [*rosso intenso, rosso chiaro, rosso e verdegiante, verde, gialle, bianche, arugine o altro colore*]; their flavors are sweet, sour, or in between [*dolce o brusche o di mezzo sapore*]; they are fragrant or not; they keep themselves for a long or a short time; their peels are smooth and polished or rough and lumpy [*scorza liscia e polita o aspera e tuberosa*]."

We find similar information also in older sources, such as *De Flore Dietarum* ("the sour apples are cooler, the sweet or fragrant ones between hot and cool and are of middle quality"), *Ruralia Commoda* (5.12), and Savonarola's book (19v-20r).

Orange. Oranges were commonly used to make compotes and candies, or as acidifiers for sauces or other dishes. We find them in few recipes, for example, in *Anonimo Veneziano*'s cookbook. In the *Registrum Coquine*, they are used to make a frittata and a sauce.

Medieval oranges were sweet, sour, or with an intermediate flavor, writes Savonarola [*alquanti sono acerbi. Alquanti tirano al dolce. Alquanti tengono il mezo sapore,* 19r]. It is hard to identify precisely the kinds Bockenheim is referring to for his recipes, but in any case, according to Savonarola, sweet oranges are the best.

Pine nuts. Pine nuts appear in many recipes since the Antiquity. In the medieval cookbooks, they are used in the same way as almonds, to garnish dishes and make milk or candies.

There are a few recipes to prepare a sort of torrone called *pinochiato* (spelled in many ways), which Platina, in the 15th century, describes as covered with golden leaves to show off luxury (23v). In the *Registrum Coquine*, they usually appear in recipes meant for the rich and nobles. One of these recipes is a *torta* finished with silver and golden leaves (27).

Almonds. In this book, almonds are mainly used to make almond milk, but in a few recipes they are added ground or whole to the dishes. In the Middle Ages, we find both bitter and sweet almonds, but the first ones are used to prepare medicinal remedies and not foods (Savonarola, 26r-26v; Platina, 23r).

Almond and pine-nut milk. Milk made with almonds and other nuts is common in medieval and Renaissance cuisine, not only as a substitute for regular milk. The preparation of *lac amigdalorum* and *pinearum* is very simple and quick. You need to use peeled almonds (or shelled pine nuts) and grind them finely in the mortar, then dilute the paste you obtained with a liquid. In many cases, it is made with water, but sometimes, medieval authors, including Bockenheim, use broth. In recipe 1, for example, the author writes to dilute the ground almonds with chicken broth.

If you prefer to buy almond milk already prepared, pay attention that it is made with just almonds, without additives that would ruin the flavor of the dish. Avoid even the ones that contain sugar: though sugar is frequently paired with almond milk, you must keep the sugar content in check not to overpower the dish with an excessively sweet flavor.

Dates and raisins. Dates and raisins are other two ingredients essential in historical cooking since ancient Rome. They appear in *De Re Coquinaria*, as well as in the medieval and Renaissance cookbooks, to prepare sauces, sweets, pies, but also meat and fish. Wines made with dates or raisins are thoroughly described in the sources.

In the Middle Ages, there were several varieties of raisins and dates. Raisins were with or without seeds. The kinds Savonarola considers better are the *passule de Corinto*, which he believes the most nourishing and helpful for the stomach, in particular if eaten with almonds (17v).

The author of *De Flore Dietarum* distinguishes between white and black raisins, the first lighter for the stomach than the latter.

3.3 Milk, cheese, and eggs

Dairy products and eggs are essential in the medieval alimentation during the fat, as well as meat. In the *Registrum Coquine* there are several meatless soups and pies with eggs and cheese.

Milk and cheese. The ancient and medieval sources describe the various kinds of milk. The most common were cow, sheep, and goat milk, as we read in Anthimus [*vacca aut capra aut ovis*, 76] and *De Flore Dietarum* (in which the author mentions camel milk too, to imitate Galen). Savonarola, in addition, mentions buffalo milk (54v).

Bockenheim, however, mainly uses almond milk (see above), with just one time regular milk in manuscript B for a pie (38). There is then a further recipe with sheep milk in manuscript A. Knowing which kinds of milk medieval cooks had at their disposal, however, help us to select the proper kinds of cheese. Bockenheim, habitually, just writes whether the cheese must be fresh or aged, without giving further explanations.

Thanks to Michele Savonarola's book (56r-57r), we know that some kinds of cheese are fresh, others aged, others half-way [*alchuno e frescho. Alchuno e antiquo. Alchuno e de mezo tipo*]. In any case, as we have seen about milk, cheese is made usually with cow, sheep, or goat milk [*alchuno de pecora. Alchuno e de vaccha. Alcuno de capra*].

We suggest reading the recipes to understand how it is used: if it must be pounded, use a firm cheese like a caciotta or a scamorza, called *provatura* in the medieval sources, but described also by Columella in his *De Re Rustica*, in a passage in which we find plenty of recipes for cheese in ancient Rome that will remain identical throughout the Middle Ages (7.8). If you need an aged cheese, try with Parmigiano or pecorino.

If the author writes to use grated cheese, you need an aged one. If you have to prepare a sweet, use a cheese with a low salt content: as Savonarola writes, cheese may be more or less salty [*alchuno salato. Alchuno e men salato*].

In addition, in the *Registrum Coquine*, butter is quite common. You find it described in the paragraph dedicated to the cooking fats.

Eggs. The most used kinds of eggs are the ones of chicken, duck, and goose, despite Savonarola (53r-54v) considers goose eggs hard to digest and suitable for peasants [*e pur e duro da padire (…) imperho e pasto da rustico*]. Also ostrich eggs are mentioned in the sources; again, frowned upon by Savonarola.

We find the eggs not only in the sources, but also in the pictures of the *Tacuina Sanitatis*. In other cookbooks, for example *Anonimo Toscano*, there are also fish eggs used during the lean days. Usually the recipes do not provide further explanation about the kind to choose, and the *Registrum Coquine* is not an exception. In any case, chicken eggs are perfectly good to make a philological dish, not to consider that the dietetic sources, for instance *De Flore Dietarum*, consider them the best along with others that may be quite hard to find: partridge and starling eggs.

There are plenty of recipes for eggs, not only in the culinary texts but also in the medical handbooks. In addition to the recipes specifically for eggs, they are used in several dishes: soups, crusts for the pies, meatballs, sauces, fillings, and others.

3.4 Meat and fish

In medieval cuisine, meat is the most important ingredient, substituted in the lean days with fish.

In the *Registrum Coquine*, there are recipes with several kinds of meat, among which birds and game. According to the author of *De Flore Dietarum* and other physicians, however, the birds have a better meat than any quadrupeds. Moreover, Bockenheim uses frequently offal to make soups or pies, but also sauces and stuffings.

The culinary tradition of the Middle Ages includes extensive explanations about the best ways to cook whichever kinds of meat. Books like the *Tractatus de Modo Preparandi et Condiendi Omnia Cibaria* or the *Libro de Arte Coquinaria* dedicate many pages to the cooking techniques, in addition to the medical handbooks.

Chicken. Chicken and capon are among the most used meats in the *Registrum Coquine*. In manuscript B, the meat appears six times, the offal once, and the broth four; in manuscript A, twice both the meat and offal. Moreover, there are three recipes for capon in manuscript B (in addition to recipe 29, in which it is probably used just the broth) and one more in manuscript A.

The proper way to cook chicken, according to Maestro Martino, is roasting it, whereas a good capon (in the same way as the hen) must be simmered or if it is well fat, roasted. A common cooking technique for chicken or capon (but also for other kinds of meats that need to be roasted) consists in simmering it briefly, then cooling it down in water, and spreading it with pounded lardo and spices. This method is more or less the same described in the *Tractatus*. Maestro Martino suggests stuffing it with herbs or fruits, then spitting the bird and cooking it at low heat, since it is essential a slow cooking.

A way, instead, to simmer chicken consists in cooking it whole for an hour with sage, hyssop, or parsley, not minced, with the addition of white wine or verjuice, writes the anonymous author of the *Tractatus*.

In the medical handbooks, we find out that chicken is considered one of healthiest kinds of meat, in particular the hen. *Gallina excedit omnia volatilia*, we read in *De Flore Dietarum*: the hen is better than the other birds. The capon is considered temperate and excellent by the physicians and cooks. It can be always substituted with chicken in the recipes, without a substantial change in the outcome.

Chicken must be eaten extremely fresh, Anthimus suggests (23): in winter, within two days [*hiberno tempore and biduum occidantur*]; in summer, before the evening [*aestivis diebus ante seram*].

Pheasant. Pheasant appears three times in manuscript B (and once more in manuscript A) in recipes for nobles and rich, except one in which it may be substituted with chicken or pigeon (17).

According to Maestro Martino, it needs to be roasted, the same opinion shared by the author of the *Tractatus*, who recalls that it must be cooked keeping it distant from the fire, without simmering it in water, in the same way as crane, partridge, and dove.

Michele Savonarola (35v-36r) writes that it is not only a costly meat, but it is unsuitable for workers who make a great physical effort as well as the poor, whereas it is fit for the convalescent and weak.

"The pheasant is a noble meat and costs too much [*il fasano e carne zentile, e tropo costa*]. Since it is rare and expensive [*rara e cara*], people want it more than capons [*la brigada* — a term that refers to common people — *la appetisse piu chel capone*]."

Patridge and starling. Partridge too is a meat for the rich [*carne da zentili, e richi homeni*], good both roasted and simmered, writes Savonarola (36r-36v). The starling is a good, temperate meat in the same way as quail, that is suitable to the convalescent, weak, and elders.

Peacock. Savonarola advises the nobles against eating peacock (36v-37r), which since the Anticuity was considered a delicacy suitable for the richest tables. The physician, instead, believes that it must be avoided by the nobles, since "it is not a food for your grace, nor for anyone who lives a refined life" [*non e cibo da tua Signoria, ne da nissuno altro che usi la vita zentile*]. It must be exclusively eaten by strong people who make great efforts [*quelli che sono robusti e de grande exercitio*].

The best way to cook peacock and remove the possible harm is to simmer it well and dust it with spices. To roast it properly, one must precook them in water previously. Peacock must be paired with good, fragrant wine [*drieto al manzare di quello se vole bevere de bon vino e odorifero*].

Bockenheim neglects these measures and in his only peacock recipe, he suggests serving the roasted meat with a peppery sauce or cooking it in its sauce directly (26).

Anthimus (24) does not share Savonarola's worries and recommends eating old peacocks within five or six days, cooking them with wine and adding honey and pepper; the younger ones, instead, must be eaten within two or three days.

Pigeon. Pigeon is another prized meat in historical cooking, since ancient Rome. Savonarola (37r-37v) suggests his liege to eat this meat once in a while, recommending it to the ones with fevers. The best way to prepare pigeons is by roasting them, because they are humid, then dressing them with a sauce made with vinegar, rose water, coriander seeds, and a bit of sugar [*manzare se voleno con il sapore fatto de aceto, acqua rosata, e specie de coriandro preparato con un pocho de zucaro*].

Maestro Martino writes that pigeon is good simmered, but roasted is better.

Duck and goose. Birds like duck, goose, crane, heron, or swan have to be roasted, after stuffing them with garlic, onions and other (unspecified) good things, writes Maestro Martino. According to Savonarola (39v-40r), ducks must be roasted and greased continuously with oil, adding garlic and good spices [*voleno essere rostite e continuamente unte de oleo, e preparate con laio e specie bone*], but wild ducks need to be pre-cooked in water.

In this cookbook, we find a recipe for goose or duck and one for goose. Differently from duck, usually goose is roasted without previously greasing it with some cooking fats, as we read in the *Tractatus:* it does not need to be greased since it is fat [*lardationem non indigent dum pinguis est*].

Other birds. In the *Registrum Coquine* we also find small birds and swamp birds. Savonarola frowns upon the swamp birds, considering them a bad meat, in particular swan that he calls a meal for fisherman [*pasto stranio da piscatore*], as well a smerganser. The small birds instead, which he calls *ocelletti de ciesa* (church small birds) are good and nourishing, in particular wrapped in vine leaves, shortly boiled, and cooked under the ash (39v; 41v-42r).

Goat and lamb. In Maestro Martino's book, we read that the meat of the young goat is good both simmered and roasted, but its back is better roasted, in the same way as lamb. Goat, instead, is good in January with a garlic sauce, whereas the wether is all good simmered, except the shoulder and leg that are excellent roasted.

The meat of the one-month-old goat is good and temperate, writes Savonarola (45r), if the animal is sufficiently grown and fat. It is a delicate meat, unsuitable for peasants. The best way to cook it consists in simmering the meat, not roasting it, adds the author, whereas Anthimus disagrees (5): goat and lamb are good cooked in all ways. Suckling lamb, Savonarola continues (45r-45v), is hard to digest, and to remove the potential harm, it must be cooked with cinnamon and rosemary. It is better the meat of the weaned lamb. The meat of the wether is good, both simmered and roasted.

Without specifying the age of the animal, Anthimus (4) considers mutton a kind of meat suitable to be eaten frequently. If roasted, it must be kept distant from the fire to prevent it from burning externally, remaining raw inside, because in this way it causes harm.

Veal and beef. The proper way to cook veal breast, Maestro Martino recommends, is by simmering it, whereas the loin must be roasted and the leg used to make meatballs. Fat cow and beef meat, instead, has to be simmered.

Veal is easy to digest and nourishing, writes Savonarola (45v-46r). The beef between one and three years, the author adds, gives good nourishment, but it is a meat suitable for workers (*artisani*) and people with a robust stomach. To make it more delicate and fit for nobles, the meat must be kept for a few days in winter to hang. Adult-bovine meat, instead, is bad and provides melancholic nourishment.

Pork and wild boar. Differently from Maestro Martino, who believes that pork is unhealthy cooked in whichever ways (but recommends roasting its back with onions and salting the rest or cooking it as one wants), the author of *De Flore Dietarum* considers that it is a good meat, well nourishing, being pork the most temperate among the quadrupeds.

Like all the other kinds of meat, its properties change depending on the age. It is a meat for a strong stomach and children [*e pasto da stomachi forti e da putti*], writes Savonarola (46v-47r). Two-month-old pig must be roasted to reduce its humidity, but the pig that is five or six months old is better.

However, in the cookbooks, pork is used in all ways: roasted, simmered, pounded to make *torte* and *ravioli*, with any kind of sauce.

Wild boar must be prepared with a lot of spices in preparations such as peppery sauce, writes Maestro Martino: the most common way in the medieval sources.

According to Anthimus (8), the fresh wild boar provides a lighter meat and the best ways to cook it are simmering or roasting it, keeping the meat distant from the fire.

Venison. Savonarola (44r-44v) specifically suggests preparing roe deer with a peppery sauce, the same kind of sauce used by Johannes Bockenheim (16), with the addition of its cooking liquids and vinegar.

According to Anthimus (6-7), both deer and roe dear have a good meat, if eaten fresh: old meat, instead, heavier and worse. The suggested cooking methods are simmering, steaming, and roasting them.

Hare. The hare, Savonarola writes (47v), is unsuitable for the nobles, but it is healthier if prepared with fresh pork or a fat hen, with the addition of rosemary, or with a broth made with vinegar and white pepper, or, again, with a peppery sauce (the kind of sauce suggested by Johannes Bockenheim) with plenty of vinegar. However, people find it more savory if roasted and well greased with lard.

Anthimus (13) suggests a kind of peppery sauce for the hare, made with pepper, a bit of cloves, ginger, costus, lavender or Indian bay leaves [*piper habente, parium cariofili et gingiber, costum et spica nardi vel folium*].

Offal. The tripe, as well as the lungs and heart, is not a food for courtiers, writes Savonarola, despite the fact that we find it frequently used in high-end recipes. The physician suggests cooking it with honey, broth, ginger, and salt (43r). The liver must be paired with wine, and the best kind is goose liver, appreciated since ancient Rome. Savonarola recommends frying it with oil and salt, adding fennel.

Anthimus, instead, suggests avoiding fried pork liver, both to the sick and people in health, but if one wants to make it, he recommends to place the liver on a grill and brush it with oil or lard, then eat it with oil, salt, and ground coriander (21).

Fish. In this cookbook, we find just a few recipes for fish, usually less appreciated than meat in medieval cuisine and considered a substitute for the lean days. Some physicians, such as the anonymous author of *De Flore Dietarum* and Anthimus, prefer freshwater fish, which is largely represented in the cookbooks; others, instead, for example Savonarola, believe that saltwater fish is better (49r-50v). Anthimus write that trout and perch are the best among the fish, but he considers excellent pike too (39-40).

Freshwater fish are viscous, adds Savonarola, and the remedy for this consists in washing them with vinegar (51r-51v). Savonarola warns against eating fried fish. To remove the harmful humors, fish must be simmered twice, the second time with the addition of vinegar, and then served with salt and cinnamon. Eel, instead, needs to be cooked in good wine or with garlic

Bockenheim recommends washing or marinating a few kinds of fish in vinegar or wine: carp (60), lamprey (63), and pike (61).

3.5 Cooking fats

Pork fatback and lard. Pork fatback, *lardum* in Latin, is one of the favorite cooking fats in the medieval recipes. It was usually cured, but sometimes it was used fresh. Some authors, for example *Anonimo Veneziano*, recommend melting it well and then straining the liquid part carefully, removing the residues.

In the *Registrum Coquine*, however, it appears few times, whereas we find more frequently lard, called in different ways: *pinguedo*, *sagimen* or *sagumen*, and *grassum*. In the medieval texts, we read that the cooks had at their disposal both unsalted and salted lard.

Michele Savonarola disapproves the use of large quantities of lard and pork fatback, which was eaten cooked in the Antiquity and early Middle Ages, as we learn from the sources (there is a recipe for *laridi coctura* in *De Re Coquinaria* and we find further information in Anthimus' book, chapter 14).

Savonarola writes (62v): "They are not to be used save to prepare other foods; they give poor and scarce nourishment and must be eaten in small quantities".

Olive oil. Differently from ancient Romans, who considered *lardum* a plebeian food and preferred olive oil, the medieval cooks used oil in high-end cooking more rarely, first of all (but not only) in the lean days. In any case, olive oil is the correct substitute for the animal fats.

If you use it instead of lardo (which gives not only sapidity, but also saltiness to the plate), remember to add enough salt. However, medieval olive oil was produced in the same way as the ancient Romans did, as we read in Pietro de' Crescenzi's book (5.19).

Butter. In this cookbook, we frequently find butter, more used than in other sources of the same period. Despite it is mentioned in the Edict of Prices issued by Emperor Diocletian, in the Antiquity, butter was considered a barbarian food (*barbarorum gentium lautissimus cibus*, Pliny, 28.133), whereas in the Middle Ages it became quite common in Italy. In the high-end cuisine, it was less used than other cooking fats; however, in the Renaissance, it was frequently used in courtly cooking.

The use of butter in the *Registrum Coquine* is particularly interesting because it is a typical German food, according to Michele Savonarola, who attributes the presence of a series of diseases among the Germans to their huge use of butter (55v). Later, Pietro Andrea Mattioli confirms that, writing that the Germans prepare a very popular food made with oats, clearly butter, and milk (2.83).

Butter can be salted or not (in the same way as lard), as we read clearly in Anthimus' *De Observatione Ciborum* (77).

In the lean days, it is substituted with olive oil, but in a few manuscripts, there are recipes for almond butter, which can be used instead, though it is not mentioned in the *Registrum Coquine*.

Almond butter. This is the method described in *Anonimo Veneziano*'s manuscript to make almond butter: "If you want to make butter with almond fat to make plates for Friday or Lent, take three pounds of almonds to make a *torta* or any dish you want for twelve people […]. In the days without meat, take well peeled, well washed, and well ground almonds [*ben monde e ben lavate e ben masenate*] and mix them with clear water in such a way the milk is well thick [*fai che sia ben stretto*], then strain it and boil this almond milk. When it is well cooked, throw it on a white cloth. When the water is well strained, remove the butter with a knife and place it on a plate, then use it for any dish you want."

3.6 Wine, vinegar, verjuice

Wine. Wine provides complexity to the dishes, with its slight acidity that depends on which one we are using. The medical sources mention several kinds of wine.

In *De Flore Dietarum*, we read that fresh wine is aged up to two years, aged wine to seven years. The aging time, clearly, changes the characteristics of the wines: "fresh wine is hot in the first degree. Aged wine that reaches the seventh year is hot in the fourth degree. Half-way wine, aged from two years to four, is hot in the second degree".

The basic colors for wine are white and black, whence come all the others: "some wines are white, others black. From these, there are made golden, red, white, and rosé wines. And then, the golden, *citrinum*, *palmeum*, and whitish [*aureum, rubeum et glaucum et etiam roseum. Item aureum et citrinum et palmeum et subalbidum*]".

The thickness changes depending on the kind of wine: there are watery, thin wines [*subtile et aquosum*] as well as dense, earthy wines [*terrestre et grossum*]; some wines are sweet [*dulce*], others sour [*acerbum*], others again have a strong flavor and smell [*forte in odore et sapore*].

In addition to grape wines, there are others, made with dates, figs, raisins, but we also find ale, considered a wine made with barley or wheat. *Anonimo Meridionale* and Savonarola (59r) write about pomegranate wine.

To simplify, we suggest red or white wine, depending on the kind of dish, when the author writes nothing about the quality of wine: if you are preparing a dish with delicate flavors, use white wine; if, on the contrary, the aromas are stronger, choose red wine.

Vinegar. The meat comforts the appetite, writes Pietro de' Crescenzi, if dressed with vinegar (4.45).

Usually, there are no directions about whether to use white or red vinegar. We suggest using it white with sauces for a delicate meat or fish, or for plates that must be yellow or white; red with meat or fish with a strong flavor.

Verjuice and unripe grapes. Verjuice is the juice obtained by unripe grapes. Its use, however, dates back to ancient Greece, and ancient Romans called it *omphacium*, from Greek *omphakion*, a word with includes unripe-olive oil.

According to Mainus de Maineris, the proper time of the year to use verjuice is summer, whereas in winter wine and vinegar are better. Other possible substitutes are acidic juices, such as lemon, orange, green sorrel, and vine-top juice, or pomegranate wine [*succus limonum citrangulorum acetum et succus viridis acedule et extremitatum vitis vinum granatorum*].

The use of unripe grapes in summer and vinegar in winter appears even in ancient Greek cuisine, as reported by Athenaeus about the recipe for *mattyes*, written by Artemidorus of Tarsus *(Deipnosophists,* 663e): a chicken plate with a sauce made, indeed, with unripe grapes or vinegar, vegetables, and *lagana*, an ancient Greek fried flatbread.

According to Pietro de' Crescenzi, there are two kinds of *agrestum*, dry and liquid [*agrestus sit duplex liquidum et siccum*, 4.25]. To make liquid *agrestum*, pick unripe grapes, pound them, and place them in the sun with salt in a basin or a vase [*pistantur et in mastellum vel tinam vel alium vas ponuntur ad sole*]. After two or three days, extract the juice and preserve it until it is used [*postquam duobus vel tribus diebus ab solem steterint, accipitur succum et repositur usui servetur*]. There are some who, the author continues, do not add salt, but in this way, the *agrestum* keeps well for a longer time.

To make dry *agrestum*, instead, harvest very unripe grapes, crush and squeeze them, then cook their juice until it is well thickened, pour the liquid in a large vase, leaving it to dry in the sun, then store it. Someone dries the juice without previously cooking it.

3.7 Spices and aromatic herbs.

Spices. In medieval cuisine we find mainly Eastern spices, whereas ancient Romans and Greeks preferred Mediterranean ones. In the *Registrum Coquine*, there are fewer spices than in other cookbooks, but they are worth to be examined.

First of all, it is important to notice that, according to Bockenheim, the spices must be used in all plates, included the ones destined to the lower classes. This is nothing new: we find the same directions in *Anonimo Toscano*'s cookbook, in which plates with saffron and other spices are clearly intended for the reader himself, possibly a professional cook, or even the servants, not for a noble.

The main difference between foods for the rich and foods for the lower classes is in the quantity and quality of spices (clearly, a lesser quantity for the plebeians) and the kind of ingredients: pigeons, pheasants, capons, pine nuts, silver and gold leaves, and other similar rich foods for the nobles; mutton, fish, garlic, leek, or bovine meat for the less rich.

The presence of spices in the foods for the plebeians must not cause surprise, in a cultural context in which they are so common. A pinch of pepper (or a few stems of saffron) is less expensive than one guesses, both at these times and today, being their weight almost insignificant. A minimal quantity, indeed, is sufficient to give a lot of flavor to a dish, with very little cost. Clearly, a huge quantity, as we find in some cookbooks for the nobles, such as *Anonimo Veneziano*, is extremely costly, and we have to consider this fact before preparing medieval dishes.

Saffron. *Crocus* or *zapharano* are the different terms (one Greek and Latin, the other Arabic) used in the two manuscripts of the *Registrum Coquine*. In other texts, we find both. This could mean the presence of different qualities of saffron available in Italy, one local and the other imported, or, in the case of the *Registrum Coquine*, just the geographical distance between the two copyists.

Pietro Andrea Mattioli (1.25), however, in the 16th century writes that *zafferano* is the Arabic name used in all Italy, but in some places, in particular the countryside of Siena, it is still used the ancient term *cruogo*, a spelling variant for Italian *croco*.

Michele Savonarola (69r) writes that it may be considered the essential ingredient to make the sauces, since without it, it seems that one can not make a good sauce [*materia prima de sapori che senza lui pare non poterli fare boni*].

Saffron is common not only in the *Registrum Coquine*, but also in all the other Italian sources, across all social classes. In *Anonimo Toscano*'s manuscript, for example, we find this recipe, meant for the servants: "take turnips simmered with their leaves and cook them with beef, pepper, and saffron [*carne di bue, e pepe, e cruoco*]. When it is cooked, serve it in plates to the common *famiglia*." *Famiglia*, in this case, has the same meaning as Latin *familia*, namely the servants working in the household.

However, it seems that saffron was very common in Germany. Mattioli, after recalling that it is widely cultivated in Italy, writes: "There is excellent saffron, better even than the one cultivated in L'Aquila, in all parts of Germany, in the archduchy of Austria, in the territory of Vienna, the main city of that province. But from that, just a small quantity is exported in Italy, because the Ungarians and Germans are reluctant to allow saffron to be taken from their countries for the great use they make of spices [*di questo pochissimo ne passa in Italia; perciocché mal volentieri gli Ungheri, e i Tedeschi per l'uso grande che fanno delle spezie, se lo lasciano cavare dal paese loro*]."

A common substitute for saffron, adds Mattioli (4.189), is carthamus, also called Saracenic saffron [*zafferano Saracinesco*].

Costanzo Felici is another author who confirms essentially, what we see clearly in the *Registrum Coquine*: that saffron is used every day in every kind of plate and that it is extremely common.

Writes Felici: "I say, it appears frequently and daily in the kitchens, as though it wants to be part of everything. Its taste and fragrance improve the other dishes and correct their defects, and then it shows its beautiful yellow color [*viene, dico, lui frequentissimo e quotidianamente nelle cucine et è tale che quasi vole entrare per tutto, contribuendo alquanto il suo sapore et odore et corregendo molti diffetti d'altre vivande e poi mostrando il suo bello colore giallo*]."

Pepper. The other spices that we find in the *Registrum Coquine* are pepper, cinnamon, cloves, ginger, and nutmeg, all known by ancient Romans (with the exception, maybe, of nutmeg), who, however, made a moderate use of them as cooking ingredients, mainly to aromatize garum and wine.

Bockenheim mentions just white and black pepper, but in the Middle Ages, also long pepper was common, used in Italy since the Antiquity. Pepper is by far the most used Eastern spice in ancient Roman and Greek recipes. In the commentary to the *Regimen Sanitatis Salernitanum*, Arnaldus de Villa Nova writes that pepper is a condiment for rustics [*salsamentum rusticorum*], which means for the people who live in the countryside, as well as garlic.

The wide use of pepper among the plebeians is confirmed, a few centuries later, by Costanzo Felici: it is used in any kind of dish and there is among the common people the saying that one who has pepper uses it even to dress a humble vegetable as cabbage [*chi ha del pevere il mette sopra cauli*].

Cinnamon. Cinnamon is another Bockenheim's favorite. Felici reports that at his times there are two main varieties of cinnamon used in any kind of plate, cooked or raw, and even in the salads like pepper: one finer, costly, and intensely fragrant; the other coarser, blander, and cheap.

Ginger. Ginger, fresh or dry, was used since the Antiquity and appears in a few recipes in *De Re Coquinaria*. In the Middle Ages, however, it was widely used in cuisine and to make candies, pills, preserves, and other medicinal remedies.

Sweet spices. Johannes Bockenheim frequently uses a blend of sweet spices, without writing more about it. From other medieval sources, we know that the spices considered sweet were cloves, ginger, cinnamon, saffron, Indian bay leaves, nutmeg.

This is the recipe that we find in *Anonimo Veneziano*'s cookbook: "1/4 of an ounce of cloves, one ounce of good ginger, one ounce of cinnamon, and a good amount of Indian bay leaves. Grind all these spices together as you like [*uno quarto de garofali e una onza de bon zenzevro e toy una onza de cinamoleto e toy arquanto folio e tute queste specie fay pestare insiema caxa como te piaxe*]."

According to *Anonimo Toscano*, instead, this is the ratio among the spices: "6 ounces of ginger, ½ ounce of cinnamon, 1 ½ ounces of cloves, 1 ½ ounces of nutmeg, 1 ounce of saffron [*çenzovo beledo o colomi* (two different kinds of ginger) *unce VI, canella fina uncia ½, garofani uncie I ½, noci moschade uncie I ½, çaffarano uncia I*]."

Mediterranean spices. In this cookbook, we find, sometimes, Mediterranean spices, in addition to saffron, mentioned before. In a few recipes, there are anise and coriander seeds as well as juniper. Differently from ancient Roman cuisine, medieval cooking prefers the strong Eastern spices to the Mediterranean ones, which are mainly suggested in the medical handbooks to make the foods more temperate.

Aromatic herbs. The text mentions a few aromatic herbs, to which we can refer each time the author writes just to add herbs. As well as for the spices, his favorite herbs are fewer than the ones a medieval cook had at his disposal. The most used in this cookbook are parsley and marjoram, then sage, rue, dill, mint, and rosemary.

Parsley is very common in medieval cuisine and appears frequently in Roman recipes. In the medieval cookbooks, we find not only the herb, but also a variety called root parsley (here in recipe 8 and the variant of recipe 4 present in manuscript A). This one, despite being still cultivated in Italy, is now rare as a cooking ingredient.

In other sources, we read lists of aromatic herbs. In Michele Savonarola's book, for example, there are entries about fennel (both the seeds and herb, but some cookbooks, such as the *Liber de Coquina*, use the white part of the fennel), celery, and arugula (both the herb and seeds, used in the same way as mustard seeds); Platina mentions cilantro, thymum serpyllus, pennyroyal, basil, lesser calamint, thyme, oregano, and others.

3.8 Honey and sugar

Honey is a fundamental ingredient in both ancient and medieval cuisine, however, in the latter, it is less used than sugar. Writes Simon of Genoa in the 13th century in his *Clavis Sanationis*, a glossary of medical terms, (42r) that honey was common in the ancient times more than at his contemporary age, and that at his times sugar is the ingredient more used to make the preserves temperate [*mel aput antiquos in usu fuit plusquam aput modernos: moderni vero zucharo magis utuntur in confecionibus temperandis*]. However, we frequently find honey in the medieval cookbooks, included in the *Registrum Coquine*.

The best way to use honey and remove most of its potential harm, writes Savonarola after Dioscorides (62v-63r), is cooking and foaming it [*per esser cosi cotto e spumato se ge tuole i nucumenti suoi in grandissima parte*], a method suggested even in the ancient recipes.

According to Galen (*De Facultatibus Simpliciorum Alimentorum*, 12.9), sugar and honey have the same properties; however, Savonarola (63r-63v) believes that sugar is more nourishing than honey [*da mazore nutrimento chal miele*]. The better kind, the author writes, is the white one cooked three times [*el migliore e il bianco de tre cotte*], a good food for the stomach. In addition to sugar, Savonarola and other authors, such as Aldebrandin of Siena, write about the so-called cane honey, used in liquid form, which has the same characteristics as honey.

In medieval cuisine, sugar is used in any kind of plate, not only to make sweets but also fish, meat, pies, and other dishes, because as Savonarola writes, it makes tastier the foods [*fa il cibo piu delettevole*], in a similar way honey is used by ancient Romans, as we read in *De Re Coquinaria*.

Costanzo Felici adds more about sugar, and his information is consistent with the way in which it is used in the cookbooks. "Sugar never ruins a soup. It is used to make food and beverages more refined, making them sweet and flavorful [*con esso si rende delicato il magnare e molte volte il bevere, facendo dolce e saporito e l'uno e l'altro*]. It appears many times in the salads and is a good pairing with vinegar, which seems to be its natural companion [*che par compagno alla sua natura*]. Sugar is used to preserve many foods for a long time and all year round. There is a substantial variety of sauces in a liquid form and dishes in a solid form at such a point that we can truly say that this is a precious aliment able to preserve well, since human nature takes great delight in this sweet flavor."

Following, the author describes the several kinds of sugar existing at his time. "There are many kinds of sugar, with various names, sold at different prices [*se ne vende di esso de più sorte con più nomi a varii prezzi*]: big pieces red and white, pyramidal cakes, many kinds of a solid and big brown variety called coarse sugar, according to the different places from where it is imported. There is the little cake called fine sugar and then the candy sugar prepared more for medicinal purpose than as a food [*se ne vende di esso de più sorte con più nomi a varii prezzi, perché o sonno rottami e rossi e bianchi, o in pani piramidali e turbinati sodi e grandi de più sorte secondo la varietà de' paesi, detto zuccaro grosso, e poi il pane piccolo detto zuccaro fino, e poi vi è il candito fatto più per medicina che per cibo*]. The varieties of sugar imported from some countries are better than others."

REGISTRUM COQUINE

RECIPES FROM MANUSCRIPT B

Incipit registrum coquine quomodo et qualiter preparantur cibaria per integrum annum, et quomodo ministra debent fieri, et diversa pulmenta. Et salsamenta que apponuntur diversis ferculis, tam pro magnatis et nobilibus quampro diversis aliis prelatis. Et personis per me Johannem Buckenhem, quondam coquum s.d.n. Martini Quinti.

It begins here the *Registrum Coquine* about in which way and how are prepared the dishes for all year round, how the soups need to be made, and the various plates. And the sauces that accompany the different dishes, both for the rich and nobles, and for different other prelates. And [I have written it] in person, Johannes Buckenhem, once cook under [Pope] Martin V.

—

In manuscript A, there is this significant variant to this text: the recipes are meant *tam pro magnatis, nobilibus et prelatis quam aliis personis*, namely for the rich, nobles, and prelates as well as for other kinds of people, which corresponds to what we find in this cookbook. Instead of *salsamenta*, moreover, the copyist writes *salsa*, which is better Latin, since *salsamenta* usually refers to salted meat or fish.

1.
AN EXCELLENT SOUP
FOR THE RICH AND NOBLES

Et primo fac ministrum optimum. Recipe amigdala et pista illa bene in mortario, et tempera illa cum bono brodio gallinarum et vitulorum ovorum. Et post recipe agrestum. Si est tempus estivale. Si autem est tempus hyemale, tunc recipe gariofolos cum cinamomo, et fac parvas petias, et mitte illas ad scutellam, et sperge superius cynamomum, cum zucharo, et erit pro magnatis et nobilibus bonum.

And first, make an excellent soup. Take almonds and pound them well in the mortar. Dilute with good chicken broth and add egg yolks. Then, take verjuice, if it is summer. In winter, cut cloves and cinnamon into small pieces, then plate them [with the soup] dusting with [ground] cinnamon and sugar. This will be good for the rich and nobles.

–

This recipe calls for almond milk prepared with chicken broth and mixed with egg yolks, probably raw, since the author uses the verb *tempera*: dilute. As common in the medieval recipes, the author follows, partially, the typical directions provided by the physicians, adding verjuice in summer. However, he does not suggest using vinegar in winter, as one would expect, but just spices.

In manuscript A, this recipe is called *ministrum de amigdalis*, almond soup.

2.
BREAD SOUP FOR THE ITALICS AND RUSTICS

Ministrum pro Italicis et rusticis. Si facis ministrum de panibus. Recipe panem grattatum, et tempera bene cum brodio grasso et cum croco ac caseo et aliis spetiebus bonis, ut spissum fiat. Et erit bonum pro Italicis et rusticis.

Soup for the Italics and rustics. Make in this way bread soup. Take grated bread and mix it well with fat broth, adding saffron, cheese, and other good spices, in such a way it becomes thick. It will be good for the Italics and rustics.

–

In other recipes, the author specifies to use *panis albus*, white bread made with wheat flour. In this case, the author writes nothing about the kind of bread. You can prepare it with wheat, millet, or barley, using flour white or with a little content of bran, being this recipe meant for people living in the countryside, kneading it with sourdough and a pinch of salt.

About the cheese, the author does not write whether it must be fresh or aged, so we suggest following your taste, as well as for the choice of spices. In any case, the broth has to be thick with bread and cheese.

3.
VEAL OR PORK FOR THE ITALICS

Ad carnes pro Italicis preparandas. Ita prepara carnes pro Italicis. Recipe carnes vitellinas vel porcinas macras et scinde in partes ad longitudinem unius digiti, et fac tot petias quot vis. Post hoc recipe granum coriandri et pista illa bene in mortario et inmitte sal. Et illas petias pone super vnam tabulam vel super unum lapidem. Et sine eas stare per horam, et post hoc mitte ad verutum et fac illas lente rostire et sperge superius illa grana pistata et erit bonum pro Italicis.

To prepare meat for the Italics. Prepare in this way meat for Italics. Cut veal or lean pork into pieces one finger long. Make how many pieces you want. After that, pound coriander seeds well in the mortar adding salt. Place these pieces under a table or stone, letting them rest for an hour. After that, spit the pieces and roast them slowly, dusting them with ground coriander seeds. It will be good for the Italics.

This is a very simple recipe for spit-roasted meat, with just coriander seeds and salt, with the suggestion by the author to use lean meat.

In manuscript A, this recipe is called *copiae*. The word and preparation recall a recipe that we find in Maestro Martino's *Libro de Arte Coquinaria*, written later in the 15th century than the *Registrum Coquine*, called *coppiette al modo romano*. The ancestor of this dish may be found in *De Re Coquinaria*, with a recipe for pork loin similar to these, since the meat is cut in half, but not completely, seasoned with pepper, minced cilantro, and fennel seeds, and then wrapped in caul fat and roasted (7.8).

It is interesting to read Maestro Martino's recipe to better understand the one by Bockenheim: "Cut the meat into pieces as big as one egg [*pezzi grossi como uno ovo*] without opening it completely [*non la fornire di tagliare*], because these pieces must remain attached the one with the other; take a bit of salt and coriander seeds, or ground fennel seeds [*un pocho de sale et de pitartema, cioè il seme di coriandri, o vero finocchio pesto*], and cover the pieces of meat with them; then place them for a while under a press [*poneli un pocho in sopprescia*] and spit-roast them, placing thin slices of lardo between the pieces to keep the meat more tender [*coceli in lo speto arrosto mettendo in esso speto tra l'uno pezzo et l'altro una fettolina di lardo sottile per tenere le diete copiette più morbide*]."

The use of slices of lardo is a good idea, because it prevents the meat from becoming too dry.

In manuscript A, we read that we have to place the meat on a table under a stone to press it for one hour [*et pone illas parte super una tabula, et pone unum lapidem superius; et mitte illas sic stare per horam*], which is equivalent to Maestro Martino's suggestion to place the meat *in sopprescia* for a while.

Differently from the version we are translating here, the other manuscript suggests this recipe for the Romans, a fact that recalls Maestro Martino's name for this recipe (*coppiette* in the Roman way).

4.
MUTTON FOR THE ALEMANNI AND GERMANS

Pro Alamanis et Germanis. Sic prepara carnes castratas. Recipe carnes et pone in aquam recentem et fac illas modicum stare donec sanguis exeat. Et tunc eas ad ignem donec sanguis exeat pone. Et quando sunt bullite tunc mitte superius et adices petrosilini, et fac modicum brodium et mitte superius crocum. Et erit bonum pro Alamanis et Germanis.

For the Alemanni and Germans. Prepare in this way mutton. Place the meat in fresh water, keeping it there for a short time until the blood oozes. Then place it on the fire until the blood oozes. When it is cooked, add parsley, make a bit of broth, and add saffron. It will be good for the Alemanni and Germans.

–

A simple and quick dish with the meat of the wether [*caro castrata*], washed and then cooked briefly, just until the blood begins to come out, with the addition of parsley and saffron.

When the author writes to make a bit of broth, he means that the blood and parsley should remain liquid, not excessively thickened.

In manuscript A, the author writes to use *radices petrocilini,* root parsley.

5.
BEEF FOR CITIZENS, RUSTICS, AND PEASANTS

Pro civibus rusticis et villanis. Sic prepara carnes vaccinas et bovinas. Recipe eas et lava bene in aqua, et fac illas bene bullire. Post hoc mitte superius annetum aut cepas cum sale et croco et modico aceto et erit bonum pro civibus rusticis et villanis.

For citizens, rustics, and peasants. Prepare in this way cow meat and beef. Wash it well in water, then boil the meat well. After that, add on top dill or onions with salt, saffron, and a bit of vinegar. It will be good for citizens, rustics, and peasants.

–

Like all medieval authors, Bockenheim distinguishes between beef and cow meat, which possess different qualities according to the directions of medieval medicine. In this recipe, the well-cooked meat is seasoned with saffron, vinegar, and dill (in the seasons in which dill is available, namely spring and summer) or onion (probably, in winter).

Manuscript A, indeed, recommends using *anetum viridis*, fresh dill, with the addition of salt, not mentioned in this variant for the recipe, and suggests this recipe for the Alemanni.

6.
PORK FOR WOMEN

Pro mulieribus. Sic prepara carnes porcinas. Recipe eas, et lava bene et mitte ad ignem. Et cum fuerint cocte, mitte superius ova cruda cum croco et cepis et aceto. Et erit bonum pro mulieribus.

For women. Prepare pork in this way. Wash the meat well, then place it on the fire. Once it is cooked, add on top raw eggs, saffron, onions, and vinegar. It will be good for women.

–

In the end of this preparation, raw eggs, saffron, onion, and vinegar are added to the pork soup before serving. We suggest beating the eggs and stirring for a few seconds, whereas the saffron must be diluted in warm water. You may choose whether to add the onions finely minced on top or to pound them in the mortar and mix them with the egg, vinegar, and saffron. In this latter case, you will obtain a general flavor more balanced, but we suggest following your taste.

In manuscript A, the author recommends this recipe *pro nobilibus villanis*: literally, for noble peasants, which does not make any sense. Probably, in this case, the author means the nobles that live in the *villae,* their country homesteads.

7.
VEAL FOR THE ROMANS

Pro Romanis. Sic prepara carnes vitellinas. Recipe eas et lava bene ut prius et spuma bene. Et quando sunt cocte tunc mitte interius uvam passam et gariofolos cum aliis spetiebus dulcibus et tempera illa cum vino et aceto, et erit bonum pro Romanis.

For the Romans. Prepare veal in this way. Wash the meat well as in the previous recipes and remove the foam [from the cooking liquid when you boil the meat]. Once it is well cooked, add raisins, cloves, and other sweet spices, and dilute with wine and vinegar. It will be good for the Romans.

–

Probably, raisins must be pounded in the mortar with the other spices, then diluted with wine and vinegar, but you can add them whole, after steeping them in warm water for at least ten minutes.

The author uses sweet spices. You find a paragraph about this blend of spices in the chapter dedicated to the ingredients.

8.
PORK SOUP FOR THE ITALICS

Bonum ministrum de carnibus pro Italicis. Sic prepara ministrum de carnibus. Recipe carnes porcinas macras bullitas, cum petrocillo et radicibus eius et pista illa cum cultello, cum pane albo grattato et mitte illa simul modicum bullire. Et erit bonum pro Italicis.

Good meat soup for the Italics. Prepare in this way a meat soup. Pound with a knife boiled lean pork with parsley and its roots. Add white grated bread and boil all the ingredients together. It will be good for the Italics.

–

In this recipe, the author uses root parsley, a variety of parsley quite common in the medieval cookbooks. If you do not have it, you can use instead just parsley, or a bit of Florence fennel, or another Apiacea, such as parsnip or celery.

The text recommends using white bread, stale since it is grated and then added to the meat and parsley pounded together with the knife, obtaining in this way a thick broth.

Manuscript A adds to the list of the ingredients *speciebus bonis*, good spices.

9.
OFFAL SOUP FOR THE ROMANS

Aliud ministrum pro Romanis. Sic fac ministrum pro Romanis. Recipe iecur et pulmonem coque et fac petias parvas et mitte eas in lacte amigdalorum cum bono brodio grasso et optimis spetiebus et buliantur insimul modicum et erit optimam.

Another soup for the Romans. Make in this way a soup for Romans. Cook the liver and lung, then cut them into little pieces. Place them in almond milk with good fat broth and excellent spices. Boil them together for a short time. It will be excellent.

—

This simple offal soup is enhanced by the presence of almond milk obtained by mixing almonds, fat broth, and spices, a delicious combination. This manuscript does not specify which kind of offal to use, whereas in manuscript A we find that they must be of simmered goat [*capritti bulliti*]. We suggest also mutton, pork, or veal offal, all used in medieval cuisine.

10.
OFFAL SOUP FOR THE ALEMANNI

Aliud ministrum pro Alamanis. Recipe pulmonem castrati aut vituli coctum, vel iecur et pista illa insimul cum cultello et tunc recipe caseum antiquum grattatum cum ovis et spetiebus et tempera illa insimul. Et fac bene bullire et erit bonum pro Alamanis.

Another soup for Alemanni. Pound with a knife mutton or veal lung, already cooked, or [cooked] liver. Then take grated aged cheese with eggs and spices and mix all the ingredients together. Boil them well. This dish will be good for the Alemanni.

–

The method is completely different from the latter: in this case, the lung and liver are pounded with the knife and mixed with grated cheese, beaten eggs, and spices, making in this way a thick soup.

This recipe does not appear in manuscript A.

11.
LIVER SOUP FOR THE BOHEMIANS AND HUNGARIANS

Aliud ministrum pro Bohemis et Hungaris. Recipe epar porci sive vituli aut agni. Et pista illa in mortario. Et mitte intus modicum mellis et aliaram spetierum dulcium. Et mitte modicum insimul bullire, cum croco et erit optimum.

Another soup for the Bohemians and Hungarians. Take pork, veal, or lamb liver, and pound it in the mortar. Add a bit of honey and other sweet spices. Boil them together with saffron. It will be excellent.

–

This dish is another thick broth with pounded liver, honey, and spices. Do not exaggerate with honey to prevent the soup from becoming excessively sweet.

Manuscript A recommends this recipe for the Alemanni.

12.
GOAT TRIPE FOR THE ITALICS

Aliud ministrum pro Italicis. Recipe intestina capreti et pista illa cum cultello cum ovis duris, et tempera illa cum brodio gallinaram, cum croco et aliis spetiebus. Et erit bonum.

Another soup for the Italics. Take goat tripe and pound it with the knife with hard-boiled eggs. Mix the tripe with chicken broth, adding saffron and other spices. And it will be good.

–

The author forgot to write that the pounded eggs and tripe must be cooked after mixing with the other ingredients (or, as an alternative, that the tripe must be precooked), but this step is easy to reconstruct from the previous recipes, very similar to this one.

Manuscript A recommends using good broth [*bono brodio*].

13.
MEAT PLATE FOR THE RICH

Aliud ministrum pro magnatibus. Recipe carnes pullorum cum carnibus bene coctis, et pista illa cum cultello cum caseo, ovis, et croco et cum aliis spetiebus. Et tunc mitte superius cynamomum. Et erit bonum.

Another plate for the rich. Take chicken meat with another well-cooked meat and pound them with the knife with cheese, eggs, saffron, and other spices. Dust with cinnamon on top. And it will be good.

—

We suggest using a cheese firm enough to be beaten with the knife. The eggs are surely hard-boiled, like in the latter recipe, being pounded with the other ingredients. This version of the recipe does not specify which kind of meat to use, in manuscript A, instead, we find *carnibus porcinis coctis*, cooked pork.

Probably, this soup is not meant to be cooked, but directly served: there are no further liquids added to the other ingredients.

14.
PIGEON OR CHICKEN
FOR THE ITALIC PRINCES AND NOBLES

Aliud ministram pro principibus et nobilibus. Recipe pipiones et pone in patellam in pinguedine lardi et cooperi bene et verte eas aliquando, quibus decoctis. Recipe amigdala. Et pista cum cultello et ova cruda temperata cum agresto postea eice pinguedinem et intus mitte aquam roseaceam. Ita quod illa temperata fiat aliquantulum spissa et totum mitte super pipiones aut pullos, et erit bonum pro Italicis.

Another soup for the princes and nobles. Cook pigeons in a pan with lardo. Cover well the pan [with a lid] and turn the pigeons once in a while until they are cooked. Pound almonds with a knife, then mix raw eggs with verjuice and add [the melted] lardo and rose water. Cook the mixture until it thickens and pour it on the pigeons or chickens. It will be good for the Italics.

–

Lardo is fundamental for this recipe, being used not only to fry the meat, but also to make the sauce. If you prefer using olive oil, remember to add a pinch of salt. The condiment is prepared with almond milk made with verjuice, eggs, and rose water, cooked until thick.

15.
CHICKEN OR PIGEON *PASTILLUM* FOR THE ITALICS

Ad parandum polastros pro Italicis. Recipe polastros sive pipiones, et fac bulire ut prius. Et quatuor vel quinque fac petias ad libitum tuum, et pone eas ad pinguedinem in patella, et videne comburatur. Et post hoc recipe maioranum, cum aliis spetiebus bonis, viridibus zinsibere, cynamomo, et ovis crudis. Et misce cum croco et agresto, et tunc fac pastam, et eam pone in tegamo et mitte omnia illa intra pastam et mitte pipiones aut polastros inferius et temperaturam illam superius et erit bonum pro Italicis.

To prepare chickens for the Italics. Take chickens or pigeons and boil them as described above. Cut them into four or five parts, as you prefer, and cook them in a pan with lard, paying attention not to burn them. After that, take marjoram with other good spices, fresh ginger, cinnamon, and raw eggs. Mix with saffron and verjuice and make a crust. Put the crust in a pan and stuff it, placing below pigeons or chickens and above this mixture. It will be good for the Italics.

For this recipe, the author suggests cooking the meat two times, a technique that, as we have seen, was quite common in the Middle Ages: first, simmer the meat, then cut it into pieces and fry with lard.

The recipe omits that this plate is a pie, probably a *pastillum*, in which the meat is placed in a crust, pouring over a mixture with raw eggs, spices, and aromatic herbs. The filling is then wrapped in the crust. The pie, then, has to be cooked in the oven, in a pan, or under a *testum*, called by the author in another passage with the Greek term *clibanus*: a dome made with terracotta or copper meant to be covered with charcoal, beneath and above, to bake bread and pies.

Manuscript A recommends this recipe for the Romans and adds lard to the mixture poured on the pigeons [*mitte illam temperaturam superius cum pinguedinem*].

16.
VENISON WITH BLACK PEPPERY SAUCE FOR THE RICH

Ad faciendum piperatam nigram pro magnatibus. Recipe carnes caprioli, et fac illas rostire in spidone, et postea fac petias parvas et pone illas in pinguedinem calidam in patella. Et fac bulire cum cepis, postea mitte hoc totum foris. Et recipe panem grattatum rostitum et fac piperatum nigrum de vino et agresto, zinzibere, garioffolis, cynamomo et pipere, et mitte intus pineas et uvam passam. Et funde super carnes et sperge et erit pro magnatibus.

To make black peppery sauce for the rich. Take roe-deer meat and spit-roast it. Then, cut it into small pieces and cook them in a pan with hot lard. Cook the meat with onions, then remove both from the fire. Take roasted and grated bread and make a black peppery sauce with wine, verjuice, ginger, cloves, cinnamon, and pepper, adding pine nuts and raisins. Pour the sauce on the meat and spread it. It will be good for the rich.

In the medieval manuscripts, there are several recipes for *piperata* or *piperatum*, a kind of sauce characterized by the presence of a great amount of pepper, black or white, and other spices, sometimes with the addition of toasted bread.

In *De Re Coquinaria*, it is a sauce with pepper and garum. Medieval *piperata* is usually paired with meat and fish with a strong flavor, in particular game meat. In this case, the sauce, poured on the spit-roasted meat cut into pieces, is prepared with bread, spices, pine nuts, raisins, wine, and verjuice.

In manuscript A, the author adds vinegar (*aceto*) to the liquids.

17.
PHEASANT, CHICKEN, OR PIGEON WITH WHITE PEPPERY SAUCE

Ad faciendum piperatum album. Recipe caseum grattatum bonum temperatum cum croco et ovis et aliis spetiebus, ac zucharo, et agresto et sale, et aqua roseacea. Post hoc recipe fasianos, seu pullos, vel pipiones et divide illos in partes ad libitum tuum. Et mitte omnia illa simul bulire modicum et erit optimum.

To make white peppery sauce. Take good grated cheese mixed with saffron, eggs, other spices, sugar, verjuice, salt, and rose water. After that, take pheasants or chickens or pigeons and cut them into pieces as you want. Cook all the ingredients together for a while and it will be excellent.

–

This, instead, is a variant for *piperatum album*. We suggest using white pepper. Pepper is not listed among the ingredients, but probably the author gave it for granted or, simply, forgot to mention it since the basic meaning of *piperatum* is pepper-based sauce. In this case, the meat is cooked directly in the sauce, made with cheese, spices, eggs, verjuice, salt, and rose water.

This recipe does not appear in manuscript A.

18.
LITTLE BIRDS FOR THE SAXONS AND DACIANS

Ad parandum aves parvas pro Saxonibus et Dachis. Recipe sturnos et omnes alias parvas aviculas, et fac illas bene bulire post hoc divide eas in quatuor partes. Et recipe capita et iecora eorum et pista illa cum iunipero et agresto, et mitte eas rostire in pinguedine et mitte illas partes intus. Et mitte superius illam coperturam, et erit bonum pro Saxonibus et Dachis.

To prepare little birds for the Saxons and Dacians. Take starlings and all the little birds and boil them well, then cut them into four parts. Pound their heads and livers with juniper berries and unripe grapes. Fry them with lard and add the parts of the birds. Serve them with this mixture on top. It will be good for the Saxons and Dacians.

–

To prepare this recipe exactly as the author meant it, it is essential using very small birds, because their crushed heads are part of the ingredients. Clearly, if you prefer to omit this part, use the meat you prefer: chicken or duck cut into pieces, or quails.

Agrestum in this case means unripe grapes, not verjuice, being pounded in the mortar with the juniper.

This is the only recipe of this cookbook in which appears juniper. We suggest adding a good amount of it since there are no other spices.

Instead of *coperturam*, manuscript A reads *temperaturam*, mixture, which makes more sense.

19.
PORK TRIPE
FOR THE SAXONS AND MARCOMANNI

Ad preparandum stomachum porci pro Saxonibus et Marchionibus. Sic prepara stomachum porci. Recipe eum et lava bene cum sale, et aqua, et post hoc recipe panem gratatum, et caseum cum petrosillo, maiorana, et spetiebus aliis, cum pipere, et pista illa insimul. Et tunc recipe ova cruda, secundum quantitatem eiusdem, et tempera illa, cum croco et aliis spetiebus et mitte intus. Et quando est coctus, tunc mitte crocum in brodium et erit bonum pro Saxonibus et Marchionibus.

To prepare pork tripe for the Saxons and Marcomanni. Prepare pork tripe in this way. Wash it well with salt and water. After that, take grated bread, cheese, parsley, marjoram, other spices, and pepper, pounding all the ingredients together. Mix raw eggs, according to the size of the tripe, with saffron and other spices, then stuff the tripe. Once it is cooked, add saffron to the broth. It will be good for the Saxons and Marcomanni.

This is a very interesting recipe for stuffed pork tripe. The filling is prepared with bread, cheese, raw eggs, aromatic herbs, and spices, yellow-colored with saffron, which is used for both the filling and broth. This is a recipe with a very long cooking time, but surely worth a try, fragrant and full of flavor.

The variant in manuscript A presents some differences. The author does not use grated bread, just grated cheese [*caseum grattatum*] and hard-boiled eggs [*ova dura*] instead of raw eggs, adding verjuice [*agrestum*]. The recipe is recommended for *Frisonibus et Slavis*.

20.
PORK LIVER FOR PIMPS AND GLUTTONOUS

Ad preparandum figatellos de porco pro lenonibus et glutonibus. Recipe iecur porcinum cum aliis intestinis et fac partes ad longitudinem unius digiti, et circunda illas partes cum rethe porchino et mitte illas ad verutum, et fac eas rostire. Et post hoc recipe speties dulces cum bono brodio grasso. Et mitte illas partes superius in scutella vel super uno disco ita quod brodium non tangant. Et sperge tunc superius speties dulces. Et erit bonum pro glutonibus et lenonibus.

To prepare pork liver for pimps and gluttonous. Cut pork liver and other offal into pieces one finger long. Wrap these parts in pork caul fat and spit-roast them. After that, take sweet spices and good fat broth. Place the liver pieces on a plate in such a way that the broth does not touch them. Dust with sweet spices. It will be good for the gluttonous and pimps.

–

Liver wrapped in caul fat and spit-roasted dates back to ancient Roman cooking. In *De Re*

Coquinaria (8.3), there is this interesting and simple recipe: "Cut the liver with a reed, steep it into garum. Grind pepper, lovage, two bay-laurel berries, then wrap it into caul fat, roast it on the grill, and serve [*ficatum praecidis ad cannam, infundis in liquamine. Teres piper, ligusticum, bacas lauri duas. Involves in omento et in craticula assas et inferes*]."

Bockenheim's recipe, clearly, is a medieval version with some typical ingredients: Eastern spices and broth.

In manuscript A, this plate is recommended for the Romans and there is the spelling variant *vigitellos* instead of *figatellos*.

21.
MUTTON LIVER FOR PEASANTS

Ad preparandum figatellos de castrone pro villanis. Recipe epar et pulmonem eorundem, et simili modo ut dictum est de porcho cum retibus eorum, et tempera ut dictum est. Licet plus debeant modicum bulire, et erit bonum pro villanis.

To make mutton liver for peasants. Take the liver and lung and prepare them with their caul fat, in the same way as written about pork liver. Then, mix them in the way mentioned above. They have to cook for a short time and will be good for peasants.

–

This is a recipe very similar to the latter, but in this case meant for peasants (in manuscript A, for the Romans) and prepared without spices.

22.
HARE WITH BLACK PEPPERY SAUCE

Ad faciendum piperatum de lepore. Recipe leporem et scortica eum ut moris est. Et cave ne sudor exeat, et fac multas partes, et lava illas cum vino et aceto. Et fac bulire istas partes cum lavatura, et non spuma, quia de ipsis fit piperatum, et si non erit satis nigrum, tunc recipe panem grattatum et mitte etiam per stamigniam. Post hoc recipe piper, gariofolos, zinziber, nuces muscatas et mitte intus uvam passam. Et erit bonum.

To make peppery sauce for hare. Take a hare and clean it as it is used. Keeping attention it does not exude liquids, cut it into many parts and wash them with wine and vinegar. Boil these parts with the washing liquid without foaming the broth, and with this liquid make the peppery sauce. If it is not black enough, take grated bread and sift it. After that, add pepper, cloves, ginger, nutmeg, and raisins. And it will be good.

–

Another *piperatum nigrum*, in this case for hare. In many medieval recipes, the blood of the hare is used to cook it, being considered since the Antiquity, in particular by Galen, a very good ingredient. In this case, the blood mixed with wine and vinegar is used to prepare the sauce.

In manuscript A, the copyist writes to use toasted bread [*panem rostitum*], which makes more sense than *panem grattatum*, if the goal is to color a sauce not black enough. In the same manuscript, the washing liquid is sifted. To the list of the ingredients, the author adds *pineas sanas*, whole pine nuts, and omits the nutmeg.

23.
DUCK OR GOOSE WITH BLACK PEPPERY SAUCE FOR THE ALEMANNI AND BOHEMIANS

Ad faciendum piperatum super aves pro Bohemis. Recipe anathem vel aucam, vel similes aves, et prepara illas ut moris est. Et mitte illas ad verutum, et sine bene rostire, post hoc fac partes, ad libitum tuum, et tunc fac piperatum nigrum ut prius dictum est cum melle, pipere, zinzibere, garioffolis et cynamomo, et insimul bulire cum carnibus, et mitte superius gariofolcs sanos, ad scutellam. Et erit bonum pro Alamanis, et Bohemis, et simili modo fac de ardea, et grue, et aliis volatilibus palustribus.

To make peppery sauce on birds for the Bohemians. Take a duck or a goose or another similar bird and prepare it as it is used. Spit-roast it without cooking the meat completely, then cut it into pieces in the way you prefer. After that, make black peppery sauce as described before with honey, pepper, ginger, cloves, and cinnamon. Cook it with the meat and add on top whole cloves when you plate it. It will be good for the Alemanni and Bohemians. In a similar way, you can prepare heron, crane, and other swamp birds.

—

In this case, the author is referring to the *piperatum nigrum* described in recipe 16, not to the latter.

The sweet ingredient added in this recipe is honey, differently from the other in which the author uses raisins. We suggest using just a bit of honey to prevent the sauce from becoming too sweet.

24.
WHITE OR BLACK PEPPERY SAUCE FOR PEACOCK FOR THE ITALICS

Ad faciendum piperatam super pavonem. Recive et munda eum, cum aqua calida. Et mitte eum rostire in veruto cum lardo bene preparatum, post hoc fac piperatum album vel nigrum ut prius dictum est. Et mitte superius, et licet aliqui solent eum cum sapore vel salsa preparare. Sic est melius pro Italicis.

To make peppery sauce on the peacock. Clean it with hot water. Spit roast it with well-prepared lardo, then make white or black peppery sauce as described above. Pour it on the meat. Someone cooks it with its flavor or sauce. In this way, it is better for the Italics.

–

The author is referring to recipes 16 and 17. This recipe can be prepared in two ways: pouring the sauce on the meat or cooking the meat with its sauce, a method that the author considers more suitable for the Italics, whereas manuscript A suggests this recipe for the Romans.

If you prefer, substitute the peacock with another bird, for example duck, goose, or chicken.

25.
BIRDS, VENISON, AND WILD BOAR FOR RUSTICS

Ad preparandum omnia alia genera avium et de porcho silvestri. Recipe de aliis avibus, iam dictis exceptis, et carnem caprioli, et fac partes et frige illas in patella in pinguedine, et tunc recipe agrestum cum modico aceto. Et impone illas partes. Et fac illas modicum bulire. Et tunc tempera illa cum bonis spetiebus. Post hoc recipe maioranam, petrosillum, et cynamomum, pista, et fac illas modicum bulire et pone intus cum uvis passis, et misce cum agresto. Et erit bonum pro rusticis. Et simili modo fac de porco silvestri sicut supra dictum est de anate, et auca.

To prepare any other kind of birds and wild boar. Take birds, except the ones mentioned above, and roe-deer meat. Cut them into pieces and fry them in a pan with lard, then take verjuice and a bit of vinegar and pour the liquids on these parts. Boil for a while, then add good spices. After this, take marjoram, parsley, and cinnamon, pound them, cook for a short time [with the meat], and add raisins, mixing with verjuice. It will be good for rustics. You can prepare wild boar in a similar way as above described for duck and goose.

—

This recipe is divided into two parts. First, the preparation of birds (except the ones mentioned before: duck, goose, swamp birds, peacock) and roe-deer meat, cut into pieces and fried with lard, then mixed with vinegar and verjuice, with the addition of spices. Following, there is the preparation of the sauce, with cinnamon, aromatic herbs, and raisins. The meat is served with its sauce.

About the wild boar, the author writes to refer to recipe 23.

26.
EASTER LAMB FOR THE RICH

Ad preparandum agnum paschalem. Recipe eum et scortica, ut moris est. Et remove omnia intestina eius, et lava bene interius, et mitte stare pedes. Post hoc recipe iecur, et pulmonem, et mitte bulire cum aliis intestinis. Et tempera omnia illa cum petrosillo et maiorana, et aliis herbis, cum lardo, croco, zinzibere, gariofolis, ovis, et caseo, et uvis passis cum sale. Et mitte totum intus, et consue bene, licet multi non inmittunt illam temperaturam et detrahe pedem unum per alium ad modum leporis, propter bene stare. Et erit optimum pro magnatibus.

To prepare Easter lamb. Clean the lamb, as it is used. Remove all the offal and wash well inside, and arrange it on its feet. After that, cook the liver and lung them with the other offal. Mix them with parsley, marjoram, and other herbs, with lardo, saffron, ginger, cloves, eggs, cheese, raisins, and salt. Stuff the lamb with this filling and stitch it well, without adding too much of the mixture, then cross the lamb's legs in the same way as it is done with the hare, in such a way it is well arranged. It will be good for the rich.

This recipe for the whole lamb is similar to stuffed roast pork and goat that you find among the recipes from manuscript A, but with more ingredients: the lamb is stuffed with a mixture of offal, herbs, lardo, spices, eggs, cheese, and raisins, probably pounded together. It is unclear whether the eggs are raw or hard-boiled, but the verb used by the author, *tempera*, means just mix; in the same way, we do not know if we have to use fresh or aged cheese. If you use the latter, grate it before adding to the mixture; a firm cheese needs, instead, to be pounded in the mortar.

The sentence *licet multi non inmittunt illam temperaturam* seems incomplete. In manuscript A we read *licet aliqui non immittunt illam temperaturam proper festum, sed solum intestina cum herbis*, which means "someone does not prepare this mixture as a filling, but just the offal with herbs."

27.
PORK *TORTA* FOR THE NOBLE ALEMANNI

Ad faciendum tortam pro nobilibus. Recipe carnes porcinas coctas et pista illas cum cultello et caseo recenti, cum zinzibere, et gariofolis, croco, et aliis spetiebus. Et tere omnia illa bene. Et tunc uva passa aliqualiter dura et eam pone in tegamo, et mitte subtus pinguedinem, ita quod non ardeat. Et mitte illam temperaturam in pastam. Et mitte superius amigdala sana aut pineas, et quando est cocta mitte superius auram et argentum propter bene stare et erit bonum pro Alamanis.

To make a *torta* for the nobles. Pound cooked pork with a knife, adding fresh cheese, ginger, cloves, saffron, and other spices. Pound all the ingredients well. Then take raisins quite dry and place them in a pan well greased with lard to prevent them from burning. Arrange the mixture in sheets of pasta. On top, add whole almonds or pine nuts. Once it is cooked, place upon gold and silver [leaves], arranged well. It will be good for the Alemanni.

Usually, *torta* is made with thin sheets of pasta, similar to lasagna, made with just flour and water, sometimes adding eggs and other ingredients. For the methods to make the dough for the *torta*, refer to the chapter dedicated to the ingredients and basic preparations.

For this recipe, meant for nobles, the author uses gold and silver leaves. We find gold to make a *pastillum* in the *Liber de Coquina*, in a recipe equally meant for the rich as a remedy for any kind of illness, with the recommendation to keep hidden from the baker the presence of gold to prevent him from stealing it.

This is the text of the recipe: "To place gold in a *pastillum*: against whichever illness, add gold in any kind of food for the rich. When you place it in a *pastillum*, make it secretly, in such a way that the baker does not change the *pastillum* [*quando ponitur in pastillo, debet fieri secrete, ne forte pastillum per fornarium cambietur*]."

Clearly, this recipe is perfectly good without gold and silver; however, golden and silver leaves are still used today as cooking ingredients.

The variant in manuscript A adds to the filling *amigdalis, datilis, et pineis* (almonds, dates, and pine nuts, in addition to the ones placed whole in the *torta*) and does not mention the cloves.

28.
MEAT *PASTILLUM* FOR THE ITALICS

Ad faciendum pastillos de carnibus. Recipe carnes quorumcunque animalium, et fac parvas petias ad modum taxillorum. Et tempera illa cum sagumine, pipere, cynamomo et croco, agresto, uva passa, cum aliis spetiebus, et fac illa modicum stare. Et interim fac pastam, et mitte eam in tegamo, et mitte illam temperatura intus totam. Et coperi bene una alia pasta, et mitte intus bonum brodium cum canella et vino mixtum. Et erit bonum pro Italicis.

To make a meat *pastillum*. Take any kind of meat and cut it into small squares. Mix with lard, pepper, cinnamon, saffron, unripe grapes, raisins, and other spices, then let the mixture rest for a while. In the meantime, prepare the crust and place it in a pan, stuffing it with the mixture. Cover the filling well with another crust and pour inside good broth mixed with cinnamon and wine. It will be good for the Italics.

–

In this recipe, the meat is marinated for a while in a mixture made with lard, spices, verjuice, and raisins. We suggest melting the lard and pound the raisins in the mortar to mix them better with the ground spices.

When you make the crust for the *pastillum*, let a hole on top, a technique frequently mentioned in other texts, including recipe 33 of this book: this is fundamental to pour liquids (in this case, broth mixed with wine and ground cinnamon) inside while the *pastillum* is baking to allow the filling to cook evenly and for a longer time without turning dry.

Manuscript A uses the variant *basteda*.

29.
MEAT *PASTILLUM*
FOR THE GAULS AND ANGLES

Ad faciendum pastillum in potto vel in pigniara. Recipe carnes bovinas vel ovinas, et fac parvas petias ut prius coctas cum grasso earundem, et si placet, mitte pipiones et alias aves in una pasta magna. Et tunc recipe cepas cum croco, et aliis spetiebus mixtas. Et mitte in patella parva, et mitte modicum agresti, cum modico brodio, et caponibus. Et mitte illas cum pipionibus modicum bulire, post hec recipe ova temperata cum bono brodio, aqua roseacea, zinzibere, croco, et cum aliis spetiebus, et pone in pasta, et quando est coctus mitte superius zuccharum, tamen aliqui imponunt caseum. Tunc erit bonum pro Gallicis et Anglicis.

To make a *pastillum* in a pot. Take pork or mutton previously cooked in their fat and cut the meat into little pieces. If you like it, place pigeons and other birds in a big crust. Then take onions mixed with saffron and other spices. Place them in a small pan adding a bit of verjuice and capon broth. Boil them with the pigeons. Then take eggs mixed with good broth, rose water, ginger, saffron, and other spices, placing them in the crust. Once it is cooked, dust the upper crust with sugar. Someone adds cheese. It will be good for the Gauls and Angles.

—

This recipe does not seem to follow the chronological and logical order of the various steps. Probably, it must be read in this way. First, choose whether to use meat (beef, goat, or mutton) or pigeons and other birds. In case you use meat, cut it into small pieces, then fry it with lard. This step is not specified for the pigeons, but possibly, they are pre-cooked in some way (boiled for a while or fried), otherwise they would not cook enough once placed in the crust. In any case, the meat or the pigeons need to be put in a big crust. The author specifies it must be big because, frequently, the crusts for the *pastillum* are quite small.

The second step consists in mixing onions (finely minced, probably, but the author says nothing about this) and spices, then cook them in a pan with verjuice and capon broth. Actually, the text reads *cum modico brodio et caponibus*, which means "with a bit of broth and capons", but it does make no sense and is probably a mistake for *brodio ex caponibus*, capon broth.

Pour this sauce on the pigeons (or meat) already arranged in the crust, then cook it (in the oven) for a while.

The author does not write about the second crust placed on top of the *pastillum*, but he probably gives it for granted, considering the following step: mix beaten eggs, rose water, and spices and pour them into the crust, probably in the same way as the recipe described above (making a hole on top of the crust to pour liquids inside during the cooking). Once the *pastillum* is cooked, dust with sugar on top. You can add cheese.

30.
PORK *BRODETTUM* FOR LAICS

Ad faciendum brodettum de carnibus pro laicis. Recipe carnes porcinas coctas et pista illas cum cultello et tempera illas cum caseo et ovis crudis, croco, et brodio grasso, et mitte in patella, et non moveas donec venit tempus prandendi. Et tunc mitte speties dulces ad scutellam pro laicis.

To make a meat *brodettum* for the laics. Pound cooked pork with a knife. Then mix it with cheese, raw eggs, saffron, and fat broth. Place the mixture in a pot, not moving it until it is time for lunch. Then serve it in plates dusting with sweet spices; for the laics.

–

In manuscript B, this recipe is called *pastillum*; however, it is completely different from the other methods for *pastillum*. The crusts are not mentioned and the recipe is very similar to the following one, called instead *brodettum* (broth), the same name with a spelling variant that we find in manuscript A, *brodittum de carnibus*. We amended the original word *pastillum* with *brodettum*.

This dish looks like a sort of savory, thick cream made with well-pounded cooked pork, cheese (probably pounded too), beaten eggs, saffron, and broth. The final outcome should be quite thick.

Manuscript A recommends this recipe for the Italics.

31.
CHEESE *BRODETTUM* FOR PRIESTS

Ad faciendum brodettum cum caseo. Recipe caseum recentem cum ovis mixtum, et mitte intus crocum cum aliis spetiebus dulcibus. Post hoc recipe brodium grassum pullorum et mitte intus, et non moveas nisi velis comedere. Tunc fac in scutellos quantum vis, et mitte superius speties; pro famulis.

To make a cheese *brodettum*. Take fresh cheese mixed with eggs, then add saffron and other sweet spices. After that, add fat chicken broth to the mixture, without moving it until you want to eat. Serve in plates the quantity you want and dust with spices; for priests.

–

This recipe is made with the same principles as the previous one and even the ingredients are the same, except for meat.

Famulus means servant, but in the Middle Ages, the meaning broadens to include the priests as servants of God. We guessed the author intended this second acceptation for the similarity with the latter recipe, suggested to laics.

Manuscript A recommends it for the Gauls and Angles.

32.
VEAL *PASTILLUM* (*PASTILLUM COMMUNEM*) FOR THE ALEMANNI

Ad faciendum pastillum communem. Recipe carnes vitellinas coctas et trita bene cum cultello et grasso eiusdem vituli, et fac pastam, et mitte eam in tegamo, et inpone speties supra pastam. Et post hoc pone carnes cum uvis passis superius cum grasso. Et quando est coctus mitte superius crocum cum vino mixtum, et erit bonum pro Alamanis.

To make a common *pastillum*. Take cooked veal and pound the meat and veal fat well with a knife. Make a crust and place it in the cooking vessel, dusting the bottom crust with spices. Then, place the meat and raisins on the crust with fat. Once it is cooked, add saffron mixed with wine. It will be good for the Alemanni.

–

A very simple *pastillum* recipe. The filling is prepared with veal, well pounded with the knife and mixed with lard and raisins. As in the previous recipes, it is essential to leave a hole on top to add, at the end of cooking, wine mixed with saffron. We recommend white wine.

Manuscript A provides the interesting suggestion to use bread dough to make this pie [*pastam de pane*], adding spices directly in the dough [*mitte species infra pasta*].

33.
PASTILLUM WITH BIRDS
FOR THE NOBLE ALEMANNI

Ad faciendum pastillum pro nobilibus Alamanis. Recipe crudos pipiones, sturnellos, et alia genera avium de palustribus et munda bene. Et recipe de carnibus vitellinis aut castrati bene tritis cum manibus ut prius. Et tunc fac pastam, et mitte in tegamo et subtus pinguedinem. Et pone carnem inferius. Et aves superius. Et mitte unum antrum. Et tempera ova, cum aqua roseacea, et croco, et mitte per antrum quando est pastillus coopertus cum una alia pasta, et erit odor suavissimus.

To make a *pastillum* for the nobles Alemanni. Take raw pigeons, starlings, and other swamp birds, cleaning them well. Then take veal or mutton well shredded with your hands as described above. Make a crust and place it in the cooking vessel greased with lard. Stuff the crust arranging the meat below and the birds above, making a hole in the crust. Mix eggs, rose water, and saffron, pouring them in the hole after covering the *pastillum* with another crust. The smell will be delicious.

This recipe requires a series of steps. First, take raw birds and clean them. Then take veal or mutton and pound it with the knife as in the latter recipe, then arrange the meat in a crust placed in a well-greased pan, placing above the birds. Let a hole in the upper crust and pour within a mixture of beaten eggs, rose water, and saffron.

Manuscript A recommends this recipe for the Angles.

34.
MEAT *PASTILLUM* FOR THE RICH

Ad faciendum pastillum pro magnatibus. Accipe capones, et pullos integros, aut divisos cum carnibus vitellinis, et avibus silvestribus, et fac pastam, et mitte aves sub carnes, cum temperatura superius nominata, in proximo, cum spetiebus dulcibus, et zuccharo, et mitte crocum mixtum cum agresto, et uva passa, mitte superius, ut purget. Et erit optimum.

To make a *pastillum* for the rich. Take capons, chickens whole or cut into pieces, veal, and game birds, then make the crust. Place the birds below the meat with the mixture described above, with sweet spices and sugar, and add saffron mixed with verjuice and raisins placed above so that they can be removed. It will be excellent.

–

This recipe is similar to the previous one, with birds arranged on pounded meat. *Temperatura*, mixture, probably refers to recipe 28: the same ingredients with the addition of sweet spices and sugar. In this case, the recipe calls for pouring inside the *pastillum* verjuice and saffron, adding on top raisins.

Manuscript A does not add in the end *ut purget*, that scarcely seems to have sense in this context, just to place raisins on top with the other ingredients.

35.
OFFAL *TORTA*
FOR THE HUNGARIANS AND BOHEMIANS

Ad faciendum tortam pro Hungaris et Bohemis. Recipe intestina agnelli, aut capretti, secundum quantitatem torte, et fac bulire, et pista illa bene cum cultello, et tempera illa cum ovis, et caseo, et aliis spetiebus, cum bono brodio, et impone cum croco. Et mitte totum in uva passa, et erit bonum pro Bohemis.

To make a *torta* for the Hungarians and Bohemians. Take lamb or goat offal, depending on the size of the *torta*, and boil them. Pound them well with a knife and mix with eggs, cheese, other spices, good broth, and saffron. Add raisins. It will be good for the Bohemians.

–

This version of the recipe does not mention the crust, whereas in manuscript A we find *una pasta* (a crust) instead of *uva passa* (raisins). There are three possible explanations: the first is that *uva passa* is a mistake by the copyist; the second is that he forgot a few words and intended to write that we have to wrap the *torta* in the crust with raisins; the third is that for this copyist, this *torta* was meant to be crustless, with raisins.

Manuscript A adds to this filling *zucharum, pineas, cum citrangulis pistis* (sugar, pine nuts, with pounded oranges).

36.
STUFFED EGGS FOR MONKS AND RELIGIOUS

Ad preparandum diversa ova pro religiosis. Recipe ova, et fac ea bulire dura. Et scortica illa, et divide per medium, et pista illa inferiora, cum petrosillo, maiorana et aliis herbis et spetiebus bonis, et imple superiora cum temperatura ista. Post hoc recipe butirum, vel oleum et calida, et mitte illa ova intus, post hoc recipe ova cruda cum agresto mixta, et vino, et petrosillo, et croco, et mitte superius,et fac omnia illa insimul bulire pro monachis et religiosis.

To prepare different eggs for the religious. Take eggs and hard-boil them. Shell and cut them in half, pounding the yolks with parsley, marjoram, other good herbs, and spices, then stuff the white with this mixture. After that, take butter or oil and hot water. Place the eggs into the liquids, then mix raw eggs with verjuice, wine, parsley, and saffron and pour this mixture above the stuffed eggs, boiling all the ingredients; for the monks and religious.

–

There are two steps to prepare this recipe. First, hard-boil a few eggs, cut them into half, and remove the yolks, pounding them in the mortar with herbs and spices. Stuff then the whites with this mixture. Do not overstuff them: the filling will swell a bit during the second cooking.

Second, cook the stuffed eggs for a short time in water and oil or butter, then add a mixture made with raw eggs, verjuice, parsley, saffron, and wine. This second cooking must be very quick to prevent the eggs from breaking; for the same reason, pay attention to mix just the liquids when you add the mixture and avoid moving the stuffed eggs too much.

Inferiora and *superiora* in manuscript A are called *rubedo* and *albedo*, yolk and egg white. There is no addition of hot water: the author just writes to melt the butter in the pan [*recipe butirum, et calefac in patella*].

37.
CHEESE *TORTA*
FOR RUSTICS, PIMPS, AND PROSTITUTES

Ad faciendum tartam pro rusticis lenonibus et eorum meretricibus. Recipe caseum frustrum unum, cum albumine ovorum, zucharo, et croco, et pone illa in pastam subtilem, et fac paulatim coquere donec indurescat. Et hoc valde lente. Et erit bonum pro rusticis lenonibus et mulieribus eorum.

To make a *torta* for rustics, pimps, and their prostitutes. Take a piece of cheese, egg whites, sugar, and saffron, stuffing a thin crust, and make it cook for a short time at low heat until it hardens. It will be good for rustics, pimps, and their women.

—

This is a cheesecake prepared within crusts and sweetened with sugar and saffron. To prepare a homogeneous filling, we suggest choosing a cheese firm enough to be pounded in the mortar, adding beaten egg whites, sugar, and saffron. The author does not mean a completely soft cheese, otherwise he would have not written *caseum frustrum*, a piece of cheese. If you want, color the dough for the crusts adding a bit of saffron diluted in water or brushing an egg yolk on top.

This recipe does not appear in manuscript A.

38.
MILK *TORTA* FOR THE SUEVIANS

Ad faciendum tortam aliam pro Suevis. Recipe lac novum, et pone ad ignem, donec coaguletur, post hoc recipe caseum novum, et tempera illa cum farina, et modicis spetiebus, et mitte illa in patellam cum butiro. Et quando est cocta, tunc mitte superius vel cum zuccharo. Et erit bonum.

To make another *torta* for the Suevians. cook fresh milk on the fire until it thickens. After that, mix fresh cheese with the milk, flour, and a bit of spices. Pour the mixture into a pan with butter. Once it is cocked, sprinkle it with sugar, and it will be good.

–

A very simple *torta* made with condensed milk, fresh cheese, a bit of flour, and spices. In this version, the copyist does not mention the crusts, but they are present in manuscript A (*magna pasta*, a big crust). The other manuscript suggests butter and lard [*segimine*], and the use of both honey and sugar [*mel cum zucarc*].

39.
CHEESE *TORTA*
FOR THE THURINGII AND HASSEII

Ad faciendum aliam tortam pro Turingis et Hasseis. Recipe caseum recentem, et dulcem, et tempera illum cum ovis, et spetiebus modicis dulcibus, et mitte in patellam, cum modico croco. Et fac valde bene coquere.

To make another *torta* for the Thuringii and Hasseii. Mix fresh and sweet cheese with eggs and a bit of sweet spices. Place in a pan with a bit of saffron and make it cook well.

–

This recipe is similar to the latter, but there are no condensed milk and flour. The crust is not mentioned, but possibly, it is given for granted.

Manuscript A suggests this recipe for the Frisians.

40.
CHEESE *TORTA* WITH SAFFRON OR HERB JUICE FOR THE SAXONS AND FRISIANS

Ad faciendum aliam tortam pro Saxonibus et Frisonibus. Recipe caseum bonum antiquum grattatum, et tempera cum ovis, et fac magnam pastam, et mitte eam in clibano, et quando est cocta, tunc mitte inferius satis de butiro, et superius mitte zucharum et crocum, sed mense Maio et Iunio cum succo herbarum, et erit suavissimum.

To make another *torta* for the Saxons and Frisians. Take aged, good grated cheese and mix with eggs. Make a big crust and place it in the *clibanum*. Once it is cooked, grease the bottom with butter enough, adding on top sugar with saffron; in May and in June, instead, add herb juice, and it will be very good.

–

A simple *torta* with grated aged cheese and eggs. Once cooked, spread butter on the bottom and dust the top with sugar and saffron. In May and June, instead, take aromatic herbs and pound them in the mortar, then sift the juice diluting it with a bit of water. In this way, however, you will obtain a soggy crust. Another possible interpretation, which makes more sense (considering that Johannes Bockenheim frequently mixes the steps up), is that the author intends that the upper crust must be prepared either with the addition of saffron or with herb juice.

The author recommends cooking the *torta* in the *clibanus*, a cooking pan with a dome meant to be covered with hot charcoal on top and below to bake pies and bread evenly, but you can use a regular oven.

41.
HERBOLATA

Ad faciendum herbolatam. Recipe herbas bonas odoriferas, scilicet petrosillum, et maioranam, mentam, et salviam, et similia et pista illa in mortario. Post hoc recipe ova cruda, et caseum recentem et misce illa cum uvis passis. Et tunc recipe crocum, zinziberem, gariofolos, nuces muscatas, et alias speties dulces, cum butiro recenti, vel oleo olivarum et fac pastam, mitte illam in patellam, et subtus et intus, pinguedinem. Et mitte illam temperaturam totam intus. Et cooperi bene, et quando est coctum mitte superius zuccharum et erit bonum.

To make a *herbolata*. Take good aromatic herbs, namely parsley, marjoram, mint, sage, and similar ones, and pound them in the mortar. After that, mix raw eggs and fresh cheese with raisins. Then take saffron, ginger, cloves, nutmeg, other sweet spices, and fresh butter or olive oil. Make the crust, place it in the cooking vessel with lard below and within. Stuff the pie with the mixture. Cover it well, and when it is cooked, add sugar on top. It will be good.

It is unclear whether this recipe is meant to be a *torta* or a *pastillum.* In any case, the dough is kneaded with lard and the filling is made with herbs (whence the name *herbolata*), eggs, cheese, raisins, and oil or butter is placed within crusts in a pan well greased with lard.

Manuscript A adds rue [*ruta*] to the list of the herbs and whole pine nuts [*pineam sanam*] on top of the pie with sugar.

42.
HERBOLATA FOR NOTARIES AND COPYISTS

Ad faciendum herbolatam aliam pro notariis et copiistis. Recipe herbas bonas, et sanas, et odoriferas, ad libitum tuum, et pista illas bene cum cultello, tunc recipe caseum recentem, cum ovis crudis temperata cum zuccharo, et croco. Post hec recipe caseum bonum, et antiquum et fac petias rotundas, et mitte super illas herbas, et mitte modicum bulire et superius zucharum.

To make another *herbolata* for notaries and copyists. Take good herbs, healthy and fragrant, according to your taste, and pound them well with the knife. Then take fresh cheese, raw eggs beaten with sugar, and saffron. After that, cut good and aged cheese into round pieces. Place the cheese above the herbs and cook for a short time, dusting with sugar.

–

This recipe shares a name with the previous one, but it is completely different. This one is clearly not a pie, but a sort of frittata. The common element is the presence of herbs, in this case not mentioned.

To chose which ones to use, we suggest referring to the other *herbolata* and to the list we made in the paragraph dedicated to the aromatic herbs.

The method is simple. Pound the herbs with the knife and mix with fresh cheese and raw eggs beaten with sugar and saffron. Place the mixture with the herbs in a pan (the author does not mention greasing the pan, but it is necessary to prevent the mixture from sticking), then arrange round pieces of aged cheese on top, sprinkling with sugar, and cook the *herbolata*.

Manuscript A recommends this recipe for copyists and their wives (*pro copistiis et eorum uxoribus*).

43.
PLATE WITH MEAT AND MEATBALLS

Ad preparandum pullos et carnes insimul. Recipe pullos, capones, et carnes porcinas, et vitellinas, et fac illas bulire insimul, et quando sunt cocte, tunc remove brodium, et serva, et recipe ova, cum micis panis albi, et mitte ad brodium, ita quod mollis fiat, post hoc recipe illa ova, et mitte per stamigniam, cum vino et aceto modico, et cum brodio; et mitte lardum ad modum taxillorum superius, et fac illa insimul bulire modicum. Et mitte totum super pullos, et carnes. Tunc fac globos de ovis et farina, carne, et uva passa cum zucharo, et aliis spetiebus, et mitte totum ad brodium, cum pullis et carnibus, et erit bonum.

To prepare chickens and meat together. Boil together chickens, capons, pork, and veal. When they are cooked, remove the broth and keep it aside. Take eggs and crustless white bread, soaking them in the broth in such a way that they become soft. Sift these eggs mixing with wine, a bit of vinegar, and broth. Add lardo cut into little squares on top and cook all the ingredients together for a short time. Pour the egg mixture upon the chickens and meat.

Then make meatballs with eggs, flour, meat, raisins, sugar, and other spices, adding them to the broth with chickens and meat. It will be good.

—

This is a recipe quite complex, with a series of steps that have to be analyzed. First, simmer the meat and remove it from its broth. The author suggests chickens, capons, pork, and veal. Cut a small piece of the meat and keep it aside to make the meatballs.

Then, steep crustless bread in a bit of broth. Mix the bread with eggs and sift them, adding wine, a bit of vinegar, and broth. Cut into small squares a piece of lardo and add them to the mixture. It must be liquid and the quantity enough to cook a bit more the meat and the meatballs that we are going to add. The author here writes to pour the mixture on the meat, but it is more logical to do the contrary: to add the meat to the broth.

Prepare the meatballs mixing eggs, flour (it is not specified which kind, but usually the authors mean white wheat flour), the meat you have previously kept aside, raisins, sugar, and spices. Add them to the broth with the meat and cook them for a while. The author does not specify if the meat for the meatballs must be cooked or raw: choose according to your preference.

We amended *uvis* (grapes) with *ovis* (eggs), the version of manuscript A, being *uvis* clearly a mistake by the copyist.

In manuscript A, sugar is substituted with saffron, and the recipe is recommended to the Angles.

44.
ROAST GOOSE
FOR THE HUNGARIANS AND SLAVS

Ad preparandum aucham domesticam. Recipe eam, et prepara ut moris est, et fac eam bene bullire, cum carnibus vaccinis. Et si placet fac eam rostire, et sanius est. Post hoc recipe alleum, et pista bene in mortario, cum micis panis, et mitte per stamigniam, et dimitte simul bulire; et mitte ad brodium anisum, et mitte illam temperaturam totam super carnes, et aucham. Sed si vis eam rostire, tunc mitte illam materiam totam intus. Et fac eam modicum plane, pro Hungaris et Sclavonibus.

To prepare the domestic goose. Prepare the goose as it is used. Boil it well with beef. If you prefer, roast it, and this method is healthier. After that, pound garlic well in the mortar with crustless bread. Sift and boil them together. Add to the broth anise seeds and pour this mixture on the meat and goose. If you want to roast the goose, stuff it with this mixture. And make it moderately stuffed; for the Hungarians and Slavs.

The author suggests two variants for this recipe, with the same ingredients. If you want simmered goose, boil it in water with beef. Prepare then a sauce pounding garlic and crustless bread, then sift and boil them with ground anise seeds, then pour this sauce on the goose.

The healthier way to cook a goose, instead, is by roasting it. In this case, stuff it with garlic, bread, and anise seeds. The copyist writes then *fac eam modicum plane*, probably a mistake for *plenam*: stuff them without exceeding, a suggestion we find frequently in the recipes that require to stuff foods.

Instead of anise seeds [*anesum*], manuscript A suggests using dill [*annetum*].

45.
PHEASANTS FOR PRINCES AND RICH

Ad preparandum fasanos pro principibus et magnatibus. Recipe eos et munda bene cum aqua calida, ut moris est. Et fac stare pennas longiores in capite, et cauda. Et mitte carnes ad aquam calidam, et mitte modicum bulire, post hoc prepara ius, cum lardo, et fac eum stare, rostire, et mitte gariofolos ad pectus, et undique, post hoc recipe pennas, et mitte eas ad caudam, propter bene stare.

To make pheasants for princes and rich. Wash them well with hot water, as it is used. Keep the longest feathers in the head and tail. Place the meat in hot water and boil for a while; after that, prepare the sauce with lardo and make them [the pheasants] stand and roast. Nail cloves in their breasts and then take the feathers and place them in their tails to make them seem nice.

–

In this recipe, the author recommends keeping the feathers aside to garnish the finished plate, quite common in the Middle Ages and Renaissance. The method is very simple: precook the pheasants in water, then stick with cloves and grease them with lardo before roasting the birds in the oven.

46.
OTHER ROAST BIRDS FOR THE MERCENARIES

Ad preparandum alias aves rostitas. Recipe aves cuiuscunque generis, et lava eas bene, et mitte illas ad spidonem ita quod aliqualiter indurescant. Tamen aliqui mittunt eas post modicum bulire. Prepara eas post hoc cum lardo ut moris est. Et quando sunt rostite, tunc mitte superius zinziberum pistum, ad scutellam. Et erit pro stipendiariis in campo.

To prepare other roast birds. Take any kind of birds and wash them well, then spit them for a short time so that they harden a little. Someone boil them for a while [before roasting]. Then prepare them with lardo as it is used. Once they are roasted, plate them adding pounded ginger. It will be for the *stipendiarii* in the field.

–

The method for this recipe is similar to the previous one. Grease the birds with lardo, then spit-roast them and serve with pounded ginger. The fact that it is called *pistum* means that probably, the author uses here fresh ginger. As a variant for this recipe, Bockenheim suggests the same method described for pheasants: simmer for a short time before roasting them.

Stipendiarii means mercenaries, but also soldiers, troops.

47.
PARTRIDGES

Ad preparandum perdices bulitas. Recipe eas, et munda ut moris est et remove intestina earum, et lava bene, et post hoc recipe brodium de carnibus vel aquam, et fac illam bene bulire. Et quando sunt cocte tunc piper ruptum per medium imponas, et simul bulire facias, et erit bonum.

To prepare simmered partridges. Clean them as it is used, removing the guts, and wash them well. After that, take meat broth or water and boil them well. Once they are cooked, add pepper broken in half and boil the meat and pepper together. It will be good.

–

In this recipe, the partridges are simmered in water or meat broth, with the addition of pepper grains broken in half. As common in the medieval recipes, salt is not mentioned, but probably is given for granted. We suggest using salted broth or water.

According to manuscript A, this recipe is good for the captains in the field [*et erit pro capitaneis in campis*].

48.
ORANGE FRITTATA FOR ACTORS

Ad faciendum fritatam de pomerantiis pro hystrionibus. Recipe pomerantias ad libitum tuum, et extrahe inde succum, et mitte ova cruda bene percussa cum zucharo, bene temperato, post hoc recipe sagimen, et fac calefieri in patella, mitte illa omnia intus, et fac plane coquere. Et erit bonum pro hystrionibus.

To make an orange frittata for actors. Take the quantity you want of oranges and squeeze the juice. Add raw eggs well beaten with sugar, well mixed, then melt lard in a pan. Add the mixture and cook it at low heat. It will be good for actors.

–

A simple frittata with orange juice, eggs, and sugar, cooked with lard. The kind of orange used by the author is probably a sweet orange, which makes sense since this frittata is prepared with sugar.

In manuscript A, this recipe is recommended to pimps and prostitutes instead of actors [*pro ruffianis et leccatricibus*].

49.
SOUP OF HONOR FOR PRINCES

Ad faciendum suppam honoris pro principibus. Recipe panem album cum ovis percussis bene, cum croco et zuccharo, et pone in pinguedine bene calida. Post hoc recipe amigdala bene pistata cum brodio gallinarum, post hoc agrestum, et impone phasanos, aut capones bene rostitos et mitte superius illam temperaturam et sperge superius cynamomum cum zucharo sufficienti, et erit pro principibus.

To make a soup of honor for princes. Take white bread with well-beaten eggs, saffron, and sugar, and fry it in hot lard. After that, take well-ground almonds with chicken broth and verjuice. Take well-roasted pheasants or capons and pour this mixture on top, dusting with cinnamon and enough sugar. It will be for princes.

–

Suppa is a plate made by placing bread on the bottom of the plate and pouring over liquids, usually broth. In this case, the soup is meant for princes, as a consequence is more complex. It is prepared in two steps. The bread, made with white wheat flour, is soaked in a mixture made with eggs, saffron, and sugar, then fried with lard. The liquid, instead, is made with almond milk prepared with chicken broth and verjuice. The author does not mention an important step, to sift the almonds, which we find in other almond milk preparations.

There is also an interesting addition to the *suppa*, roast pheasants or capons (instead of capons, manuscript A recommends pigeons). We suggest preparing them in the same way as described in recipe 45.

This *suppa* is prepared by arranging the fried bread on the bottom and the birds whole or cut into pieces on top, then pouring the liquids and dusting with ground cinnamon and sugar.

In manuscript A, this recipe is meant for kings [*pro regibus*].

50.
CHEESE SOUP FOR THE ROMANS

Ad faciendum suppam casatam pro Romanis. Recipe panem grattatum, et mitte ad scutellam, et pone superius caseum grattatum antiquum, et bonum cum spetiebus dulcibus. Et tunc iterum recipe panem et cum spetiebus donec scutella repleatur. Et tunc recipe bonum brodium grassum et mitte superius. Et iterum panem et caseum cum spetiebus; et nuncupantur apud eos Maccharone pro Romanis.

To make cheese soup for the Romans. Take grated bread and place it on plates. Add on top aged, good grated cheese with sweet spices. Then, arrange bread and spices until you have filled the plate. Pour on top good, fat broth, and then bread and spices. Among them [the Romans] it is called *maccharone*. For the Romans.

–

Another *suppa*, simpler than the previous one, prepared with cheese. In this case, arrange on the plate layers of grated bread, grated aged cheese, and spices until you have filled the plate. Pour over fat broth and finish with another layer of bread and cheese. The author concludes telling that this kind of preparation is called *maccharone* by Romans. Actually, in the texts of the same period, *maccharone* is a kind of pasta, but also a soup.

Maccus, est pulmentum ex semola et butiro (*maccus* is a plate with semolina and butter), writes Theophilus Folengus in a note to his satirical poem *Baldus* (15th century). The origin of this term, however, is Greek. *Makaira*, according to Hesychius (5th century) is a soup of flour and broth.

51.
MEATBALLS ON CHICKENS
FOR THE SAXONS AND MARCOMANNI

Ad faciendum globos super pullos pro Saxonibus et Marchionibus. Recipe uvam passam et illam lava bene cum vino et aqua post hoc recipe carnes porcinas aut vitellinas, et trita bene cum cultello, et tempera illas cum ovis et farro, croco, et aliis spetiebus dulcibus, et mitte intus uvam passam sanam et fac globos parvos et mitte illos modicum bulire in aqua, et mitte super pullos ad brodium et buliantur insimul. Et erit pro Saxonibus et Marchionibus.

To make meatballs on chickens for the Saxons and Marcomanni. Wash the raisins well with wine and water. Then, pound pork or veal well with the knife. Mix the meat with eggs, spelt, saffron, and other sweet spices and add whole raisins, shaping small meatballs. Boil for a while in water and add them to the chickens in the broth, cooking them together. It will be for the Saxons and Marcomanni.

–

This method recalls recipe 43, but a simpler version. In this case, the author uses *far* (spelt) to make the meatballs instead of flour. Probably, he means the kind of preparation that Romans called *alica*, used for example to make Cato's *globi* (79), the same term used by Johannes Bockenheim for meatballs. This kind of preparation continued to be common throughout the Middle Ages.

To make *alica*, the spelt is husked and coarsely pounded without reducing it into flour, then whitened. In Cato's recipes, *alica* is soaked into water before mixing it with the other ingredients, in this case with cheese.

We suggest doing the same with this *far*: coarsely grind it, then soak it into water overnight before mixing with eggs (the author does not specify whether to use raw or hard-boiled eggs), spices, and pounded meat. Then, stuff the meatballs with raisins washed with water and wine. Simmer the meatballs in water and cook them with chickens.

Another suitable method is to pre-cook the spelt before preparing the meatballs.

Manuscript A recommends this recipe *pro Saxonibus et Frisonibus*.

52.
EGGS WITH BROTH FOR MONKS

Ad preparandum ova cum brodio pro monialibus. Recipe ova cruda mixta cum vino et farina et mitte per stamigniam, post hoc tempera illa cum croco et sale et aliis spetiebus et fac illa modicum bulire. Et tunc mitte ad scutella ova bulita dura divisa, et mitte illam temperaturam supra, pro monialibus.

To prepare eggs with broth for monks. Mix raw eggs with wine and flour, then sift them. Add saffron, salt, and other spices, then cook the mixture for a short time. After that, plate hard-boiled eggs cut into half and pour this mixture on top. For monks.

–

Another egg dish for monks, in addition to the stuffed eggs described in recipe 36. In this case, the author writes the method to prepare a cooked sauce made with a mixture of beaten eggs, wine, and flour, sifted and mixed with spices and salt, meant to be poured on hard-boiled eggs cut in half.

Manuscript A, instead, suggests eggs moderately cooked [*ova modicum cocta*].

INCIPIT REGISTRUM COQUINE IN QUADRAGESIMA.

Here begins the *Registrum Coquine* for Lent

53.
LEEK SOUP FOR RUSTICS AND PEASANTS

Ad faciendum ministrum de porro pro rusticis et villanis. Recipe porrum album et lava eum bene et fac eum modicum bulire et trita eum cum cultello, et tempera eum cum lacte amigdalorum et modico oleo olivarum et mitte intus zucharum cum sale, tunc mitte superius cynamomum, si est extra xlam potest fieri cum bono brodio grasso cum diversis carnibus et erit bonum pro rusticis.

To make leek soup for rustics and peasants. Take the white part of the leek and wash it well, boiling it for a short time. Mince it with the knife and mix with almond milk and a bit of olive oil, adding sugar and salt, then sprinkle with cinnamon. If it is not Lent, you can prepare it with good fat broth made with different meats. It will be good for rustics.

Despite this recipe is meant for Lent, the author adds a variant for the fat days, as common in the medieval cookbooks, in which meat broth substitutes almond milk.

The method is very simple: use just the white part of the leek, boiling and pounding it with the knife, and mix it with almond milk and olive oil, adding salt and sugar, then serve with ground cinnamon.

In manuscript A, the author adds grated bread, olive oil, and saffron to the leeks and almond milk [*mitte intus oleum olive, et panem grattatum, cum zapharano*]. The recipe, in this case, is for canons and vicars.

54.
SPINACH FOR THE ITALICS

Ad faciendum ministram de spinatiis pro Italicis. Recipe spinatium, et lava bene, et mitte modicum bulire. Et tunc remove aquam, et pista illa, cum cultello, et tempera ea cum lacte amigdalorum et fac pulmentum. Deinde recipe sagimen, vel oleum olive, et erit bonum pro Italicis.

To make spinach soup for the Italics. Wash the spinach well, then boil them. Remove the water and pound them well with the knife, mixing with almond milk and making a mash. Add lard or olive oil. It will be good for the Italics.

–

In this case, the difference between the lean and the fat version is the use of lard or olive oil. The final outcome of this recipe is a mash of spinach mixed with almond milk.

In ancient Rome, the word *pulmentum*, originally, referred to the plate that accompanied the *puls*, which could be meat, fish, or even vegetables, whereas *puls* was a dish with cereals overcooked with water or milk. This *pulmentum* is a side dish for any kind of cereal preparation, including bread.

In manuscript A, the author writes to add olive oil, mixing with hot water and a bit of spices [*mitte intus oleum olive, et tempera illum con aqua callida, et modicum de speciebus*].

55.
PEA SOUP FOR THE ALEMANNI

Ad preparandum suppam de pisis pro Alamanis. Recipe pisa et mitte ea in aqua, donec fiant tenues, et tunc fac ea bulire cum aqua currente. Post hoc recipe crocum, et tempera illa cum aliis spetiebus, et mitte intus cepas ad modum taxillorum, et tempera cum oleo olive, vel sagimine, maiorana et aneto, et tunc recipe panem album, et fac parvas petias, et funde hoc totum superius pro Alamanis.

To make pea soup for the Alemanni. Steep the peas in water until they become soft, then boil them with spring water. Take saffron and mix with other spices. Add onions cut into small cubes and mix with olive oil or lard, marjoram, and dill. Then take white bread and divide it into little pieces. Pour the soup on the bread. For the Alemanni.

–

Another *suppa*, in this case meant for the lean days, with the suggestion to substitute olive oil with lard in the fat days. The author uses dry peas, soaked in water (a step unnecessary for some kinds of peas), and simmers them, adding spices, onions, oil, and aromatic herbs. The soup is then poured on white wheat bread cut into small pieces.

Manuscript A recommends toasting the bread.

56.
HEMP SOUP FOR THE SICK

Ad preparandum ministrum de canapo pro infirmis. Recipe canapium, et munda bene, cum aqua calida, et mitte eum lente bulire, ita quod coaguletur superius, et tunc superiorem partem remove et mitte per stamigniam ut aqua exeat, et tunc mitte ad ignem cum pane grattato, et cepis rostitis in oleo et tempera illa cum lacte eorum et croco, et aliis spetiebus bonis, et sperge superius uvam passam ad scutellam pro infirmis.

To prepare hemp soup for the sick. Clean hemp seeds well with hot water, then boil them until they rise on top. Remove and sift them to drain the water, then cook with grated bread and onions fried in oil, mixing with hemp milk, saffron, and other good spices. Plate and add on top raisins. For the sick.

–

The hemp seeds are husked with hot water and cooked until the seeds float on top. They are then removed and sifted, keeping aside the liquid part that will be used later to dilute the soup. The seeds are then mixed with grated bread and onions fried with olive oil, diluting with the liquid, with the addition of spices, saffron, and raisins.

57.
SPELT SOUP FOR THE SICK

Ad faciendum ministrum de farris pro infirmis. Recipe ea et fac bulire, et munda prius bene in aqua, et tempera bene illa cum lacte amigdalorum, et mitte intus crocum cum aliis spetiebus bonis, et sperge superius uvam passam ad scutellam pro infirmis.

To make spelt soup for the sick. Boil the spelt after cleaning it well in water. Mix it well with almond milk, adding saffron and other good spices. Plate adding raisins on top. For the sick.

—

Cereals in medieval cuisine have to be overcooked. In this case, the author recommends husking the spelt then simmer it, mixing with almond milk and spices. When you plate the soup, add raisins.

We amended the original *variis* with *farris*, from manuscript A, clearly a mistake made by the copyist.

Manuscript A recommends using sweet spices and adding eggs if it is a fat day [*si est tempus, potes inmitte ova*], suggesting this recipe for the weak [*pro debilibus*].

58.
FAVA-BEAN SOUP
FOR CLERICS AND RELIGIOUS

Ad faciendum ministrum de fabis pro clericis et religiosis. Recipe fabas et munda eas in aqua tepida, et fac illas stare per noctem, post hoc buliantur in aqua fluviali, et quando sunt cocte, tunc trita illas bene, et recipe vinum album, et mitte intus, et sperge super cepas cum oleo olive, vel butiro cum croco pro clericis et religiosis.

To make fava-bean soup for clerics and religious. Clean the fava beans in warm water, then soak them in water overnight. Boil them in river water. Once they are cooked, pound them well and pour white wine. Add on top onions with olive oil or butter with saffron for clerics and religious.

–

This recipe is for dry fava beans, soaked in water overnight before using them. It is unclear whether the onions and oil are added raw or if a passage is missing and the onions have to be fried in oil.

Manuscript A recommends this recipe *pro lulhardis et peregrinis:* Lollards and pilgrims. The Lollards were heretics, so it seems quite strange a recipe for them in a book written by an ecclesiastic who worked at the court of the pope.

SEQUITUR REGISTRUM DE PISCIBUS
Here follows the *Registrum* of Fish

59.
ROASTED OR SIMMERED SALMON

Recipe salmonem, et divide eum in tres partes, ita quod dorsum eius maneat sanum. Tunc fac partes ad longitudinem trium digitorum et per quam libet partem temperaturam baculum, ita quod non flectatur. Et tunc lava illas partes, et mitte ad graticulam cum sale, et quando sunt rostite, tunc perfunde partes cum succo salmonis et maiorana. Sed si vis eum bulire, tunc mitte intus vinum cum petrocillo, et erit bonum.

Cut the salmon into three parts in such a way that its back remains whole. Then cut pieces three fingers long and fasten the salmon with a stick in such a way that it does not bend. Wash these pieces and roast them on the grill with salt. Once they are roasted, pour the cooking liquids of the salmon and marjoram. If you want to simmer the salmon, add wine and parsley, and it will be good.

Like many fish recipes, the two described here are very simple, with a few ingredients: just fish, salt, and marjoram if the fish is roasted; wine and parsley to simmer it.

Instead of salmon juice, which seems to be a mistake by the copyist, manuscript A reads *suco salvie vel maiorano*, sage juice or marjoram.

The other manuscript recommends this recipe *pro Renensibus*.

60.
CARP

Ad preparandum carpones. Recipe eos et depone squamas, et fac partes, et lava in vino et aceto et mitte illam lavaturam per stamigniam, et mitte super pisces, et non spuma, et move semper cum cocleari, post hoc recipe piper, gariofolos, et zinziber, cum aliis bonis spetiebus, et mitte superius, licet aliqui buliant eos solum cum vino, et petrosillo et butiro vel oleo.

To prepare carps. Remove the scales, then cut them into pieces, washing with wine and vinegar. Sift this liquid and pour it on the fish [then cook it]. Do not foam it, but stir all the time with a spoon. After that, sprinkle on the fish pepper, cloves, ginger, and other good spices. Someone boil the carps with just wine, parsley, and butter or oil.

–

Two recipes for carps. For the first, clean the fish, cut it into pieces, and marinate it with wine and vinegar. Use this liquid to cook the fish, adding spices. For the second, boil the fish with wine, parsley, and oil in the lean days or butter in the fat days.

According to manuscript A, this recipe is suitable *pro divitibus rusticis,* for the rich who live in the countryside.

61.
PIKE

Ad preparandum luceum. Recipe eum et divide per medium, et cave ne intestina eius rumpantur. Et fac partes, et pone eas in aceto, et post hoc fac eas bulire in aqua recenti et spuma bene, et mitte superius vinum et sal cum modico de suo brodio, et erit bonum.

To prepare pike. Take it and cut into half, paying attention not to break the guts. Cut it into pieces and soak them in vinegar. Then make the fish boil in fresh water foaming it well, then [plate and] add on top wine, salt, and a bit of its broth, and it will be good.

–

This recipe requires that the fish, cut into pieces, is marinated in vinegar for a while before boiling it. It is then seasoned in a very simple way, with just wine, salt, and a bit of its cooking broth.

This and the following recipe do not appear in manuscript A.

62.
PEPPERY SAUCE ON FISH FOR THE RICH

Ad faciendum piperatum super pisces pro divitibus. Recipe pisces cuinscunque quantitatis, et fac parvas petias, et mitte in farinam, et post hoc mitte in oleo olive in patella, et fac eas bene rostire. Post hoc fac piperatum nigrum, sicut prius dictum est, et fac eas insimul bulire, et impone modicum de melle, et funde super pisces. Pro divitibus.

To make peppery sauce on fish for the rich. Take the quantity you want of fish and make little pieces, then dust them with flour and roast them well in a pan with olive oil. After that, prepare black peppery sauce as described above and boil it with a bit of honey. Pour the sauce on the fish. For the rich.

–

Use any kind of fish for this recipe, cut into small pieces. Dust them with flour and stir-fry them in olive oil. Do not exaggerate with the oil, since it will be part of the sauce. Then prepare a *piperatum* (refer to recipes 16, 17, and 23) and cook it with the fish and a bit of honey.

63.
ROAST LAMPREY

Ad rostiendum lampredam. Recipe eam viventem et vinum album, et mitte eam in caldari et quod in vino moriatur, et fac eam bulire cum eodem vino. Et tunc remove eam et mitte in scutellam, et mitte ad latus ambarum partium satis de gariofolis sanis, et pone eam ad craticulam, et fac eam rostire, et tunc unge eam cum bono brodio grasso, et mitte superius cynamomum, et erit bonum, et fac super lampredam piperatam sicut prius est dictum de piscibus.

To roast lamprey. Take the fish still alive and drown it in white wine poured in a pot. Simmer it in the same wine, then remove the lamprey from the pot and place it on a plate, sticking whole cloves on both sides [of the lamprey]. Place the lamprey on the grill and roast it, brushing the fish with good, fat broth, then dust on top with cinnamon, and it will be good. Pour on the lamprey the peppery sauce described above about fish.

–

To drown the lamprey in wine is unnecessary for a good outcome of this recipe, but it seems that it was a rather common way to dispatch eels and lampreys in the Middle Ages. You can just take your fish and clean it (a step omitted by the author), then marinate it in wine for a while. Roast the fish with cloves, pouring over a bit of fat broth and cinnamon, and serve it with a *piperatum* (again, see recipes 16, 17, 23, and 62).

If you want to make a lean version of this recipe, substitute meat broth with fish broth or the wine in which you have cooked the lamprey.

64.
COMMON BREAM FOR THE MARCOMANNI

Ad preparandum barnias. Recipe eas et mitte foras intestina, et lava ea bene, et fac partes ad libitum tuum, et tempera aquam cum vino, et tunc fac eas bullire, cum croco, et aliis spetiebus dulcibus. Et cum petrosillo, et modico oleo olive vel butiro cum agresto. Sic prepara. Recipe eas et mitte foras intestina, et lava bene et trita cum cultello illa intestina, cum maiorana, petrosillo, et uvis passis et aliis spetiebus, et mitte supra pisces, quando est coctas et erit bonus pro Marchionibus.

To prepare common bream. Take the fish and remove the offal. Wash it well and make pieces the size you prefer, then mix water and wine and boil it, adding saffron, other sweet spices, parsley, a bit of olive oil or butter, and verjuice.

Prepare them [the offal] in this way. Take the fish and remove the offal, then wash well and pound them with a knife with marjoram, parsley, raisins, and other spices. Pour this mixture on the fish when it is cooked. It will be good for the Marcomanni.

—

This recipe is divided into two parts. First, remove the offal from the fish. Cut the fish into pieces and boil it into a mixture of water, wine, spice, parsley, olive oil or butter, and verjuice.

To prepare the sauce, pound with the knife the offal and mix them with herbs, spices, raisins, and parsley pounded well together.

This recipe does not appear in manuscript A.

65.
FISH *PASTILLUM*

Ad faciendum pastillum de piscibus. Recipe pisces magnos bene coctos, post hoc amigdala, cum dactilis, et pineis, et pista illa cum croco, et gariofolo et uvis passis et trita illa cum manibus, ita quod fiant aliquater dura, et impone amigdala, pineas sanas, in pasta in tegamo, et subtussatis de pinguedine, et cave ne sit nimis de igne. Et tunc impone pisces, et fac sic illud modicum coquere pro nobilibus.

To make a fish *pastillum*. Take big fish, well-cooked, then take almonds, dates, and pine nuts, pounding them with saffron, cloves, and raisins. Knead the ingredients with your hands until you obtain a paste quite hard, then add almonds and whole pine nuts. Place the filling in a crust on a cooking vessel and cook it with lard below, keeping attention there is fire enough. Place the fish on the *pastillum* and cook it for a while. For nobles.

—

This *pastillum* is made with just one crust, with the addition of a filling made with nuts and dry fruit and whole precooked fish. The cooking time is short: as soon as the crust is done, the *pastillum* is too. For this reason, we suggest to make a crust not excessively thick.

If you want to make it for the lean days, make the dough with flour and water, adding as an option olive oil or almond butter, and substitute the lard with olive oil to grease the cooking pan.

In manuscript A, the author adds saffron to the filling, with dates instead of whole pine nuts [*inpone datilis*].

66.
SPINACH FOR THE ITALICS

Ad rostiendum spinacia pro Italicis. Recipe spinacium et lava multum bene, et mitte in patellam cum oleo olive, et move semper quod non ardeat. Post hoc mitte superius sal cum modico aceto, et sperge superius speties dulces ad scutellam. Et erit bonum pro Italicis.

To cook spinach for Italics. Wash the spinach very well, then place them in a pan with olive oil stirring all the time to prevent them from burning. Add on top salt with a bit of vinegar, dusting with sweet spices on the plate. And it will be good for the Italics.

–

Another recipe for the lean days, prepared with just spinach cooked with olive oil and dressed with salt, vinegar, and spices.

67.
NIGELLA SOUP
FOR THE BOHEMIANS AND SUEVIANS

Ad preparandum git pro Bohemis et Svevis. Recipe ea et fac bulire successine, ita quod sint tenues, et tunc removue aquam, et tempera illa cum lacte amigdalorum cum modico croco et erit bonum pro Bohemis et Svevis.

To prepare nigella for the Bohemians and Suevians. Boil the nigella until it becomes soft. Then, discard the water and mix it with almond milk and a bit of saffron. It will be good for the Bohemians and Suevians.

–

A lean soup with cooked nigella seeds mixed with almond milk and saffron. The variant for this recipe in manuscript A is with rice. You find it below, among the recipes from the other manuscript.

68.
EELS FOR THE MARCOMANNI

Ad preparandum anguillas pro Marchionibus. Recipe anguillam et scortiga eam, et fac bene bulire, et mitte superius petrocillum, cum croco, et aliis spetiebus, sed si vis eam rostire tunc divide eam per multas partes, et mitte illas partes in spidone. Et inter partes illas, mitte folia salvie, et humecta illas cum rore marino pro Marchionibus.

To prepare eels for the Marcomanni. Skin the eel, then boil it well and add on top parsley, saffron, and other spices. If you want to roast it, cut it into several pieces and spit them. Between the pieces, arrange sage leaves and moist them with a twig of rosemary. For the Marcomanni.

–

Two easy recipes for eels. To prepare the first, simmer the cleaned eel, then plate with parsley and spices, after diluting a bit of saffron in water; for the second, cut it into several pieces and spit them, alternating with sage leaves.

69.
APPLE *TORTA* FOR PEASANTS

Ad faciendum tortam de pomis pro villanis. Recipe poma diversorum saporum et scortiga, et scinde per medium ut hostie, et ea mitte in pastam subtilem, et tempera illa cum croco et aliis spetiebus dulcibus, et fac illa rostire in oleo olive, et mitte superius mel pro villanis.

To make apple *torta* for peasants. Peel apples with different flavors, cutting them in the middle as hosts. Arrange them in a thin sheet of pasta and mix with saffron and other sweet spices, then roast them in olive oil adding honey on top. For peasants.

–

A simple *torta* for the lean days made with a thin crust and filled with just apples, cooked with olive oil and spices. The author recommends using different varieties of apples, which means sweet and sour apples colored in different ways, to obtain an excellent flavor.

70.
GARLIC SOUP FOR THE RUSTICS IN THE FIELDS

Ad faciendum ministrum de alleo pro rusticis in campo. Recipe alleum et munda bene et fac illas petias bulire, et tunc mitte eas ad patellam, et frige eas cum oleo olive. Et tunc mitte intus bonum brodium cum modicis spetiebus. Et erit suavissimum pro rusticis in campo.

To make garlic soup for the rustics in the fields. Clean well the garlic, boiling its cloves. Place them in a pan to fry with olive oil, then add good broth and a bit of spices. It will be very good for the rustics in the fields.

–

This soup is intensely aromatic, with garlic stir-fried in olive oil as the main ingredient, and then spices. If you want a variant for the lean days, use fish broth or almond milk.

This recipe does not appear in manuscript A.

71.
SAUCE
FOR CITIZENS, RUSTICS, AND NOBLES

Ad faciendum salsam pro magnatibus. Recipe petrosillum, maioranam, rutam, mentam, et salviam, cum citrangulis, et trita illa omnia insimul per stamigne ammitte, tunc tempera illa cum modico vino, et aceto, et fac intus zinziber, cum croco et erit bonum pro civibus, rusticis et nobilibus.

To make a sauce for the rich. Pound together and sift parsley, marjoram, rue, mint, and sage with oranges. Mix with a bit of wine and vinegar, adding ginger and saffron. It will be good for citizens, rustics, and nobles.

–

An excellent sauce with the juice extracted from aromatic herbs, mixed with wine, vinegar, spices. We suggest pairing it with a roast, for example pork or lamb.

We amended the original term *triangulis* (which does not make any sense) with *citrangulis*, a kind of orange, possibly sour orange, which appears instead in manuscript A. In the other text, among the spices added at the end, there is cinnamon.

72.
ALMOND SAUCE FOR THE ALEMANNI

Ad faciendum aliam salsam de amigdalis pro Alamanis. Recipe amigdala, et pista illa bene, post hoc recipe zinziber et agrestum cum modico pane albo, et trita illa omnia insimul cum cultello pro Alamanis.

To make another almond sauce for the Alemanni. Pound well the almonds; after that, take ginger and unripe grapes with a bit of white bread. Pound all the ingredients together with a knife. For the Alemanni.

–

An almond sauce simple and delicious, with just ginger as a spice. It pairs perfectly with roast quails or pheasants.

In this case, *agrestum* refers to the unripe grapes, since they are pounded with the knife.

Manuscript A recommends this sauce for prelates.

73.
ANOTHER SAUCE
FOR THE RICH AND PRINCES

Ad faciendum aliam salsam pro magnatibus et principibus. Recipe uvam passam, et mitte illam ad aquam calidam, cum cortice panis albi prius positi in vino rubeo, et trita illa cum gariofilo, zinzibero, et nuce muscata, et tempera illa insimul cum agresto et valebit pro principibus et magnatibus.

To make another sauce for rich people and princes. Place in hot water the raisins with white-bread crust previously soaked in red wine. Pound them with cloves, ginger, and nutmeg, mixing with verjuice. It will be good for princes and rich people.

–

A strongly-spiced sauce, perfect for game meat, in particular wild boar.

74.
SAUCE TO KEEP THE ORGANS IN HEALTH

Salvia, sel, vinum, crocus, ruta, petrosillum. Ex hiis fit salsa que tenet precordia sana.

Sage, salt, wine, saffron, rue, parsley. With them, you can make a sauce that keeps the organs in health.

–

The last recipe of this book is intended as a sort of universal medicinal remedy. It is perfect with many kinds of plates, from roasts to simmered meat or fish.

This short recipe seems to be written along the same lines as the one that we find in the *Regimen Sanitatis Salernitanum* (21): *Salvia, sal, vinum, piper, allia, petroselinum, ex his fit salsa, nisi sit commixtio falsa* (sage, salt, wine, garlic, parsley: with these it will be made a sauce, if their mixture is not false).

RECIPES FROM MANUSCRIPT A

1.
PHEASANT OR CAPON FOR THE PRINCES AND BARONS

Aliud ministrum pro principibus et baronibus. Recipe phasanos aut capones, et fac illa bulire, ita quod manent integre. Post hoc recipe lac pinearum, et flores amigdalorum, et fac illa bulire ad modium brodii albi, ita quod erit spissum, cum zucaro et jincibero, ita quod tercia partes erit zucarum. Et mitte totum super phasanos aut capones, et sparge superius cinamomum. Et erit optimum.

Another soup for the princes and barons. Simmer pheasants or capons in such a way that they remain whole. After that, boil pine-nut milk and almond flowers in the same way as to make a white broth. When the broth will be thick, add sugar and ginger. Sugar needs to be the third part. Pour the broth on the pheasants or capons and sprinkle with cinnamon.

You can substitute the capon with chicken and pine nut milk with almond milk, obtaining an excellent dish anyway. It is more difficult to find a substitute for almond flowers, very hard to obtain without having an almond tree. You may use other flowers instead, for example orange or lemon flowers, or just skip this ingredient, added to make this rich dish more delicate and fragrant.

Brodium album means white broth and is a specific medieval preparation, considered particularly healthy: all the ingredients, indeed, are white, with just a bit of color given by the ground cinnamon.

2.
ROAST PORK FOR THE RICH

Sic debes assare porcum. Recipe intestina eius, scilicet jecorem et pulmonem, et pista illa cum cultello, et tempera illa cum ova dura, lardone, et petrocilino, maiorano, et uva passa, et speciebus dulcibus. Et tunc scinde porcum per latus, et mitte ad spitonem, et inmitte illam temperaturam, et consue bene latus; et trahe unum pedem per alium, propter bene stare, et fac valde plane rostire. Et erit pro divitibus.

Roast the pork in this way. Pound its offal, namely the liver and lung, with the knife, adding hard-boiled eggs, lardo, parsley, marjoram, raisins, and sweet spices. Cut the pork on one side and spit it, stuffing with this mixture, and stitch well. Arrange one foot on the other, in such a way that it is properly placed, and make it roast well. It will be good for the rich.

–

An excellent recipe for whole roasted pork, stuffed with its offal, still raw, and a mixture of eggs, lardo, aromatic herbs, raisins, and spices. It is easy to prepare, but the cooking time is very long. If you prefer, you can use the same ingredients to make a sauce for just a piece of roast meat, diluting with a liquid ingredient, for example verjuice or vinegar.

3.
ROAST GOAT FOR THE ITALICS

Sic assabis caprittum. Recipe intestina eius, jecorem, et pulmonem, et intestina pullorum, et pista illa insimul, cum petrocilino, maiorano, uva passa, et japharano, et cum ovis coctis et crudis, cum aliis speciebus; et mitte totus intus, et consue, et mitte ad spitonem. Et quando est cocto, recipe ova percussa, et mitte superius, cum zapharano. Et erit pro Italicis.

Roast the goat in this way. Pound its offal, liver and lung, and chicken offal with parsley, marjoram, raisins, and saffron. Add raw and cooked eggs and other spices. Stuff the goat with this filling and stitch, then spit-roast it. When it is cooked, brush with beaten eggs and saffron. And it will be for the Italics.

–

A recipe similar to the previous one, with a filling made with offal, herbs, raisins, spices, and eggs, both cooked and raw. Once stuffed the goat, stitch and spit-roast it, then coat with beaten eggs and saffron. We suggest continuing to cook for a short time and then serving it.

4.
CHICKENS FOR THE NOBLES

Sic prepara pullos. Recipe eas et munda bene ut moris est, et fac eas bulire. Et tunc mitte intus uva passa, cum zapharano, et aliis speciebus dulcibus, et mitte petrocilinum ad scutellam. Et erit pro nobilibus.

Prepare chickens in this way. Clean the chickens well as it is used, then simmer them. Then add raisins, saffron, and other sweet spices, with parsley on the plates. And it will be for nobles.

–

A recipe very simple and easy to make, with just chicken, raisin, spices, and parsley.

5.
SPIT-ROASTED ALMOND MILK FOR PROSTITUTES

Sic fac rostire lac amigdalorum in spitone. Recipe lac bene spissum, et tempera illud cum bono brodio. Post hoc recipe unam spongiam, et mitte eam in spitonem, ita quod calefiat; et tunc infunde illud lac, et volve spitonem valde lente, donec lac indurescit; et tunc divide spongiam in duas partes, et manet lac in spitone; et tunc volve spitonem lente, donec sit coctum. Et erit bonum pro meretricibus.

Spit-roast almond milk this way. Mix well-thick [almond] milk and good broth. Then spit a sponge to warm it. Pour the milk [on the sponge] and spin slowly the spit until the milk hardens. Cut the sponge into two parts keeping the milk [on the spit] and spin the spit slowly until it is well cooked. It will be good for prostitutes.

–

This is an interesting recipe with an ingenious technique. You need a natural sponge, broth, and almonds. Grind the almonds in the mortar, diluting with a bit of broth, then sift the liquid. Then spit the sponge and warm it on charcoal, pouring the almond milk a bit at a time on the sponge, until it hardens a bit. Cut the sponge into half in such a way the hardened milk remains on the spit, then finish cooking it.

6.
TURNIPS FOR PEASANTS

Sic prepara rapas. Recipe eas, et munda illas, et micte eas bulire; et tunc remove aquam, et pista illas bene, et tempera illas cum oleo olive, et lacte amigdalarum; et tunc mitte intus zucarum, cum zapharano, et sale; et sparge superius cinamomum. Et si est extra quadragesima, potest fieri cum brodio grasso de diversis carnibus. Et erit pro villanis.

Prepare turnips in this way. Clean and boil the turnips. Drain the water and pound them well, mixing with olive oil and almond milk. Add sugar, saffron, and salt, dusting with cinnamon on top. If it is not Lent, you can prepare the turnips with fat broth made with different meats. And it will be for peasants.

–

A very simple recipe for mashed turnips in which the author suggests substituting the almond milk with broth in the fat days.

7.
RICE FOR THE ALEMANNI

Sic prepara rysum. Recipe, et lava, et fac ea bulire successive, donec erint tenues; tunc remove aquam, et tempera illa cum lacte pecorum, aut amigdalarum, cum zapharano. Et erit bonum pro Almanis.

Prepare rice in this way. Clean and cook it until it is tender. Discard the water and mix the rice with sheep or almond milk, adding saffron. It will be good for the Alemanni.

–

This recipe is very similar to the one for nigella soup (manuscript B, recipe 67). As common to prepare rice, it is previously boiled in water, then cooked with milk, in this case, adding saffron.

8.
STOCKFISH
FOR THE THURINGII, HASSEII, AND SUEVIANS

Sic prepara stocbisch. Recipe eum, et mitte eum stare in aquis per noctem, quod mollis fiat. Et tunc fac eum modicum bulire, et eice aquam, et munda eum bene; et tunc fac eum plene bulire, cum cepis, et petrocilino; et tunc mitte superius zapharanum, cum aliis speciebus bonis. Et erit pro Thuringis et Hassis et Svevibus.

Prepare in this way stockfish. Soak it in water overnight until it softens, then boil it for a while and discard the water, cleaning it well. Cook it well with onions and parsley, then add saffron on top and other good spices. It will be for the Thuringii, Hasseii, and Suevians.

–

The author recommends steeping the stockfish in water overnight, but the times may be longer depending on the kind you are using.

9.
ANOTHER SAUCE FOR NOBLES

Alia salsa sic fiat. Recipe jecinora, pulmonem, et pectora pullorum, et fac illa insimul bulire, et pista illa in mortorio, cum zapharano, et modico aceto. Et erit pro nobilibus.

Another sauce is made in this way. Take chicken livers, lungs, and breasts, then boil and pound them in the mortar with saffron and a bit of vinegar. It will be for nobles.

–

A typical medieval sauce with chicken offal and meat, well pounded and mixed with saffron and a bit of vinegar, perfect for a roast or simmered chicken.

GLOSSARY

Acetum: vinegar.

Agnus: lamb. *A. Paschalis*: Easter lamb.

Agrestum and *agresta*: unripe grapes or verjuice, unripe-grape juice used as an acidifier.

Alleum: garlic. Classical Latin: *alium* or *allium*.

Amigdala: almond. In classical Latin, usually spelled *amygdala*, from Greek.

Anas: duck. In Ms A, it appears *anneta*.

Anguilla: eel.

Anisum: anise seeds.

Annetum or *anetum*: classical Latin *anethum*, dill.

Antrum: hole made in a pie to pour liquids.

Aqua: water. *A. rosacea*: rose water. *A. calida* or *calida*: hot water.

Ardea: heron.

Ardeo: to burn.

Argentum: silver.

Auca: goose.

Aura: classical Latin *aurum*, gold.

Avis: bird. Diminutive form *avicula*. *Avis* or *volatilis palustris*: swamp bird. *A. silvestris*: wild bird. *A. parvum*: small bird.

Barnia: common bream.

Brodium: Italian *brodo*, broth. *B. grassum*: fat broth.

Bulio or *bullio*: to boil.

Butirum: butter.

Calefacio: to warm.

Calidus: hot. *Calida*: hot water.

Canapus: classical Latin *cannabis*, hemp.

Capo: capon.

Capriolus: classical Latin *capreolus*, roe deer.

Caput: head.

Caro: meat. *C. vitellina*: veal meat. *C. porcina*: pork. *C. castratina* or *castrati*: wether meat. *C. bovina*: beef. *C. agnina*: lamb. *C. caprioli*: roe-deer meat. *C. cocta*: cooked meat.

Caseus: cheese. *C. recens*: fresh cheese. *C. dulcis*: sweet cheese. *C. antiquus*: aged cheese.

Castratus: neutered animal. Usually the term refers to the wether.

Cauda: tail.

Cepa: onion.

Cibaria: foods, but the author uses it as synonymous with dishes. In classical Latin, it is more common *cibus*.

Cinamomum or *cynamomum* or *canella*: cinnamon.

Citrangulum: a kind of orange.

Clibanus: an ancient portable oven covered with a dome, used to bake bread and pies.

Coclear: spoon. Classical Latin, *cochlear*.

Coctus: cooked.

Coriandrum: coriander. Ms A: *galandria*.

Crocus: saffron.

Cultellum: diminutive form from *cultrum*, knife.

Digitus: finger.

Epar: liver.

Estivalis: classical Latin *aestivalis* or *aestivus*, adjective referred to summer.

Faba: fava bean.

Far: spelt.

Farina: flour. Usually, the term refers to wheat flour, sifted to remove the bran.

Ferculum: plate, dish.

Figatellus: medieval diminutive form from *ficatum*, liver. In Italian, *fegatello*. Ms A: *vigitellus*.

Fritata: Italian *frittata*, from the Latin verb *frigo*, to fry.

Fundo: to pour.

Gariofalum, *gariofolum*, or *garioffolum*: from Greek *karyophyllon*, cloves.

Git: nigella seeds.

Globus: meatball.

Granus: grain.

Grassus: Italian *grasso* (from classical Latin *crassus*), fat, but also lard.

Graticula: classical Latin *craticula*, grill.

Grattatus or *gratatus*: Italian *grattato*, grated.

Gruis: crane.

Herba: herb. *H. odorifera*: aromatic herb.

Herbolata: ms A *herbulatum*, herb pie or frittata.

Hyemalis: wintry.

Iecur or *jecur*: liver.

Ignis: fire.

Inferius: below.

Integrum: whole.

Intestinum: intestines, tripe.

Iuniperus: juniper.

Lac: milk. *L. novum*: fresh milk. *L. amigdalorum*: almond milk. *L. pinearum*: pine-nut milk.

Lampreda: lamprey.

Lapis: stone.

Lardum: pork fatback.

Lavatura: washing liquid.

Lepus: hare.

Luceus: classical Latin *lucius*, pike.

Macer: lean.

Mel: honey.

Menta: mint.

Maioranum or *maiorana*: marjoram.

Mica: crustless bread.

Ministrum: dish, Italian *minestra*. The classical Latin

verb *ministro* means to serve at the table.

Modicum: classical Latin *modice*, moderately.

Mortarium: mortar.

Mundo: to clean, but referred to cereals, it means also to remove the husks.

Nux muscata: nutmeg.

Oleum: oil. *O. olivarum* or *O. olive*: olive oil.

Ovum: egg. *O. dura*: hard-boiled eggs. *O. cruda*: raw eggs. *O. piena*: stuffed eggs. *Albumen ovis*: the white of the egg.

Panis: bread. *P. albus*: white bread. *P. grattatus*: grated bread. *Cortex panis*: crust. *Mica panis*: crumbs.

Pasta: dough or crust. *P. subtilis*: thin crust.

Pastillum: a kind of pie made with thick crusts. Ms A: *basteda*.

Patella: pan.

Pavo: peacock.

Pectus: chest.

Penna: feather.

Perdix: partridge.

Pes: foot.

Petium: Italian *pezzo*, piece.

Petroselinum or *petrocillum* or *petrosillum* or *petrocilinum*: parsley.

Phasianus or *fasianus*: pheasant. Ms A: *phansanus*.

Pineum: pine nut.

Pinguedo: fat, usually lard.

Piper: pepper.

Piperata: peppery sauce. *P. alba*: white peppery sauce. *P. nigra*: black peppery sauce. Ms A: *pipereatum*.

Pipio: pigeon.

Pisto: to pound.

Polastrus: diminutive form for *pullus*; young chicken. Ms A: *pollastra*.

Pomum: apple. In classical Latin, the term refers to various kinds of fruit, whereas the apples are called *mala*.

Porcus or *porchus*: pork. *P. silvestris*: wild boar.

Porrum: leek.

Pottus: pot.

Pullus: chicken. In the medieval texts, we find also the diminutive form *polastrus*.

Pulmentum: originally, the foods served with ancient Roman *puls*, overcooked and mashed cereals. In the Middle Ages, the term refers to both the main and side dishes, in opposition to bread and cereals.

Pulmo: lung.

Rapa: turnip.

Rethis: caul fat. In this text, it is masculine or neuter, whereas in classical Latin it is spelled *retis* and is feminine. *R. porchinum*: pork caul fat. Ms A: *retha*.

Ros marinus: rosemary.

Rosteo: Italian *arrostire*, to roast but also to cook.

Ruta: rue.

Rysum: Ms A, rice.

Sagumen or *sagimen*: lard.

Salsa: sauce.

Salsamentum: in classical Latin, foods kept in brine, in particular fish and meat (*salsamen* is salted meat), from *sal*, salt. In Ms B, we find this term as a synonymous with *salsa*.

Salvia: sage.

Sanus: healthy or whole.

Sapor: flavor, but the term is sometimes used as a synonymous with sauce.

Scutella: Italian *scodella*, plate.

Spergo: to dust.

Spetia: medieval Latin, spice. Italian *spezia*.

Spinatium or *spinacium*: medieval Latin, spinach.

Spito or *spido*: Italian *spiedo*, spit.

Spumo: to foam.

Stomachus: tripe.

Sturnus or *sturnellus*: starling.

Succus: juice.

Superius: above.

Suppa: soup. *S. casata*: cheese soup.

Tabula: table.

Taxillus: small square.

Tegamum: cooking pan, from Greek *teganon*, Italian *tegame*. Ms A: *tegale.*

Temperatura: mixture, filling.

Tempero: to mix, to dilute.

Torta: a kind of pie with thin crusts.

Tero: to pound, to mince.

Uva: grapes. *U. passa*: raisins.

Verutum: classical Latin *veru*, spit.

Vinum: wine. *V. album*: white wine. *V. rubeum*: red wine.

Zapharano: ms A, saffron.

Zinsiber, zinziber: ginger. In Ms A, also *jinciberus.*

Zucharum or *zuccharum* or *zucarum*: sugar.

INDEX

Introduction	3
1. *The Registrum Coquine*	5
1.1 The manuscripts	6
1.2 Recipes and social classes	9
1.3 Lean days and fat days	13
2. *The other sources for this book*	17
2.1 Ancient sources	19
2.2 Cookbooks	20
2.3 Dietetic books and other sources	21
3. *Ingredients and basic methods*	25
3.1 Cereals and seeds	25
Bread	26
Torta and *pastillum*	29
Spelt	32
Rice	33
Nigella and hemp seeds	33
3.2 *Vegetables, legumes, and fruit*	35
Garlic	35
Onion	37
Leek	38
Turnip	39
Spinach	40
Peas	41
Fava beans	41
Fruit	43
Apple	43
Orange	44
Pine nuts	45

Almonds	45
Almond and pine-nut milk	45
Dates and raisins	46
3.3 *Milk, cheese, and eggs*	47
Milk and cheese	47
Eggs	49
3.4 *Meat and fish*	50
Chicken	50
Pheasant	52
Partridge and starling	53
Peacock	53
Pigeon	54
Duck and goose	54
Other birds	55
Goat and lamb	55
Veal and beef	56
Pork and wild boar	57
Venison	58
Hare	58
Offal	59
Fish	60
3.5 *Cooking fats*	60
Pork fatback and lard	60
Olive oil	61
Butter	62
Almond butter	63
3.6 *Wine, vinegar, and verjuice*	64
Wine	64
Vinegar	65
Verjuice and unripe grapes	65
3.7 *Spices and aromatic herbs*	67

Spices	67
Saffron	68
Pepper	71
Cinnamon	71
Ginger	72
Sweet spices	72
Mediterranean spices	73
Aromatic herbs	73
3.8 *Honey and sugar*	74
Registrum Coquine	79
Recipes from manuscript B	81
1. An excellent soup for the rich and nobles	83
2. Bread soup for the Italics and rustics	85
3. Veal or pork for the Italics	87
4. Mutton for the Alemanni and Germans	90
5. Beef for citizens, rustics, and peasants	92
6. Pork for women	94
7. Veal for the Romans	96
8. Pork soup for the Italics	97
9. Offal soup for the Romans	99
10. Offal soup for the Alemanni	100
11. Liver soup	101
12. Goat tripe for the Italics	102
13. Meat plate for the rich	103
14. Pigeon or chicken	104
15. Chicken or pigeon *pastillum* for the Italics	106
16. Venison with black peppery sauce	108
17. Pheasant, chicken, or pigeon	110
18. Little birds for the Saxons and Dacians	112
19. Pork tripe for the Saxons and Marcomanni	114

20. Pork liver for pimps and gluttonous	116
21. Mutton liver for peasants	118
22. Hare with black peppery sauce	119
23. Duck or goose with black peppery sauce	121
24. White or black peppery sauce for peacock	123
25. Birds, venison, and wild boar for rustics	125
26. Easter lamb for the rich	127
27. Pork *torta* for the nobles Alemanni	129
28. Meat *pastillum* for the Italics	132
29. Meat *pastillum* for the Gauls and Angles	134
30. Pork *brodettum* for laics	137
31. Cheese *brodettum* for priests	139
32. Veal *pastillum* (*pastillum communem*)	141
33. *Pastillum* with birds for the noble Alemanni	143
34. Meat *pastillum* for the rich	145
35. Offal *torta* for the Hungarians and Bohemians	147
36. Stuffed eggs for monks and religious	149
37. Cheese *torta* for rustics, pimps, and prostitutes	151
38. Milk *torta* for the Suevians	153
39. Cheese torta for the Thuringii and Hasseii	154
40. Cheese *torta* with saffron or herb juice	155
41. *Herbolata*	157
42. *Herbolata* for notaries and copyists	159
43. Plate with meat and meatballs	161
44. Roast goose for the Hungarians and Slavs	164
45. Pheasants for princes and the rich	166
46. Other roast birds	168
47. Partridges	170
48. Orange frittata for actors	171
49. Soup of honor for princes	172
50. Cheese soup for the Romans	174

51. Meatballs on chickens	176
52. Eggs with broth for monks	178
Registrum Coquine for Lent	179
53. Leek soup for rustics and peasants	179
54. Spinach for the Italics	181
55. Pea soup for the Alemanni	183
56. Hemp soup for the sick	185
57. Spelt soup for the sick	187
58. Fava-bean soup for clerics and religious	188
Registrum de piscis	190
59. Roast or simmered salmon	190
60. Carp	192
61. Pike	194
62. Peppery sauce on fish for the rich	195
63. Roast lamprey	196
64. Common bream for the Marcomanni	198
65. Fish *pastillum*	200
66. Spinach for the Italics	202
67. Nigella soup for the Bohemians and Suevians	203
68. Eels for the Marcomanni	204
69. Apple *torta* for peasants	205
70. Garlic soup for the rustics in the fields	206
71. Sauce for citizens, rustics, and nobles	207
72. Almond sauce for the Alemanni	209
73. Another sauce for the rich and princes	210
74. Sauce to keep the organs in health	211
Recipes from manuscript A	212
1. Pheasant or capon for princes and barons	212
2. Roast pork for the rich	214
3. Roast goat for the Italics	216
4. Chickens for the nobles	217

5. Spit-roasted almond milk for prostitutes	218
6. Turnips for peasants	220
7. Rice for the Alemanni	221
8. Stockfish for the Thuringii, Hasseii, and Suevians	222
9. Another sauce for nobles	223
Glossary	225

Printed in Poland
by Amazon Fulfillment
Poland Sp. z o.o., Wrocław